Mad About Muffins

Mad About Muffins

Angela Clubb

Clarke, Irwin & Company Limited
Toronto/Vancouver

Copyright © 1982 Angela Clubb

Canadian Cataloguing in Publication Data

Clubb, Angela, 1949-
  Mad About Muffins

ISBN 0-7720-1420-5
1. Muffins. I. Title.
TX769.C48   641.8'15   C82-094996-5

Published by Clarke, Irwin & Company Limited.

Printed in Canada
Design by Keith Abraham
Cover photograph by Tom Tsuji

3 4 5 G 86 85 84 83

Contents

Introduction

This book is dedicated to all muffin lovers.

The muffin, once called a "little muff" — to keep the hands warm — or a "gem," has long been a favourite in North America. Although it shares the name with the English muffin, it bears little resemblance to the flat yeast muffin baked on a griddle. Years ago, every Englishman knew of the muffin-man — both from the familiar children's ditty and the sound of his bell as he wandered through the streets selling his wares. Today there remains but one muffin-man, supplier to Buckingham Palace.

Happily, the North American version thrives. Made from a cake-like batter baked in the oven, it is similar in shape to a cupcake. Ideal for those seeking highly nutritious, easy-to-prepare food, it is enjoying increasing popularity. No longer are you restricted to the humble little bran muffin. Buckwheat, wheat germ, nuts, dried fruits, yogurt are widely available and make interesting and nourishing ingredients for both sweet and savoury varieties. Try serving them as an alternative to dinner rolls or bread; encourage your children to enjoy them as snacks. It is the joy of innovation that has made baking muffins so much fun for me. I hope this book will inspire you to experiment and discover new delights.

After baking more than 4,000 muffins (often with unpredictable results), I am still fond of them. I am indebted to my family and friends who assisted me by cheerfully consuming most of them.

My thanks to Susan Walker for her ideas and encouragement.

A *note about metrication*:
All recipes in this book are given in both imperial and metric measures. The metric measures are not exactly equivalent to the imperial counterparts, but have been rounded off to standard metric measuring units. However, the basic proportion of ingredients remains unchanged.

Simple Step-By-Step Guide

Muffins can be prepared within 10 to 20 minutes and baked in 20 to 25 minutes using the following simple steps:

1. *Preheat oven.* Most muffins are best when baked at 400°F (200°C). Make sure your oven rack is placed in the middle.

2. *Prepare muffin pan.* Grease aluminum pan or fill with paper liners. A Teflon pan requires no greasing.

3. *Assemble ingredients.* Place all ingredients on your counter top or working area.

4. *Pre-melt, pre-chop, pre-grate, etc.* Have your ingredients chopped and grated beforehand. If you have a food processor, use it to purée, grate fruits and vegetables, mash bananas, chop dried fruits and herbs etc. A blender is also useful in preparing ingredients.

5. *Assemble utensils.* Place on your working area:
  - one large bowl, approx. 10-inch (250-mm) diameter
  - one smaller bowl, approx. 8-inch (200-mm) diameter
  - a set of measuring cups — for accuracy, do not use 1 cup (250 mL) size to measure ¼ cup (50 mL)
  - a set of measuring spoons
  - a wire whisk or fork
  - one spatula
  - one large spoon

6. *Measure wet ingredients.* Add egg(s) to bowl together with sugar, oil and liquid, and combine well with wire whisk or fork. It is not necessary to beat this mixture. However, if you are doubling the recipe, place the wet ingredients in the bowl and beat briefly with a hand mixer or low speed of the electric mixer. This is helpful when combining an egg/oil/molasses/honey mixture or peanut butter mixture. Add fresh fruits or vegetables (e.g. grated carrot or zucchini/courgette) or dried fruits (e.g. apricots, dates etc.) to wet ingredients and set aside while mixing dry ingredients. This allows time for

8

fresh produce to release juices, dried fruits to soften, currants or raisins to plump, or bran, wheat germ or cornmeal to absorb liquid.

If you are adding chopped nuts to the wet ingredients, do so at the last moment, after dry ingredients have been measured, to prevent sogginess.

7. *Measure dry ingredients.* Scoop unsifted flour lightly into measuring cup and level off with a spatula. Do not level off flour by shaking the cup. It will pack the flour and increase the quantity. The result will be a heavier, drier muffin. Add leaveners and spices and stir mixture well.

8. *Combine wet and dry ingredients.* Add the dry ingredients all at once to the wet ingredients, and fold together gently. Mix only until the flour is just incorporated. Consistency of the batter will vary with the recipe, but the texture will be lumpy.

9. *Spoon batter into muffin pan.* This can be done fairly quickly as muffin tops do not have to be perfectly rounded or uniform. Add a topping before baking or place pieces of fruit or nuts on top for a decorative touch.

10. *Bake.* Place pan in middle oven rack in one layer only for even heat circulation. To prevent damage to metal, do not let pan touch side of oven. Test with toothpick or cake tester to ensure that muffins are fully baked (toothpick should come out dry and clean).

11. *Remove muffins from pan within 10 minutes.* Let cool slightly on wire rack before serving. Some muffins (e.g. Apple Cheddar, Sweet Potato) are at their best flavour when served fully cooled, while others (e.g. Cornmeal Tomato, Onion Parsley) are more delicious when served very warm.

A *proper batter*
- appears lumpy in the bowl and falls in lumps off the spoon
- produces a baked muffin with an even texture with no large holes or tunnels
- a moist and tender muffin

An *overmixed batter*
- brings out the gluten in the flour, making the dough smooth and elastic
- stretches into strands when lifted with a spoon
- produces an uneven texture with holes and tunnels
- produces a tough and dry muffin

Helpful Hints

- Choose a solid well-constructed muffin pan. It should have beaded, rounded, corners, and the cups should be seamless.

- Shiny muffin pans reflect heat whereas dull or dark pans absorb heat. Dull pans result in a browner crust and you may wish to lower your temperature by 10°F (12°C).

- Muffins are sized by measuring the diameter of the widest portion.
  miniature muffin: 2 inches (approx. 50 mm)
  medium muffin: 2¾ inches (approx. 70 mm)
  large muffin: 3½ inches (approx. 90 mm)

- When doubling a recipe, cut back on seasonings such as salt, cinnamon, ginger, cloves, nutmeg, etc. When a single recipe calls for 1 tsp. (5 mL) seasoning, adjust to 1½ tsp. (7 mL) for a double recipe.

- If using non-instant milk powder as a substitute for milk, put dry powder into the dry ingredients mixture and the required amount of water into the wet mixture. This prevents milk powder from becoming lumpy.

- To keep crusts from burning, always try to leave one muffin cup partially filled with water. The vapour will prevent burning. This also avoids uneven baking.

- If you have only enough batter to fill half of the muffin pan, fill the remaining cups with water to avoid heat damage to the metal.

- Before freezing muffins, allow them to cool fully. Wrap in foil or place in air-tight plastic containers or plastic bags. Suggested storage time for frozen muffins is one to two months.

- To reheat frozen muffins, cover lightly with foil and place in a 400°F (200°C) oven for 25 minutes.

- Muffins are best eaten within two days of baking. Store in a container with a loose-fitting top. Muffin tops can become sticky or too moist in an air-tight container.

- To reheat muffins, cover lightly with foil and heat in a 400°F (200°C) oven for 10 minutes, or place in a brown paper bag, sprinkle the outside with water and bake at 300°F (150°C) for 20 minutes.

- To freshen stale muffins, sprinkle water on inside of a paper bag, fill with muffins, close bag tightly and bake at 300°F (150°C) for 20 minutes.

- Leftover stale muffins may be frozen in a plastic bag and used later as a quick topping for a casserole. Crumble frozen muffins on top of a casserole, dot with butter and sprinkle with cheese. This is especially good when done with savoury or whole-wheat muffins.

- Grease pan for savoury muffins with leftover bacon grease.

- To grease a muffin pan quickly and avoid messy fingers, slip hand into a plastic sandwich bag, then grease.

- If you like to make extra large muffins, grease the top of the muffin pan. This will prevent the muffin tops from sticking to the pan.

- To clean encrusted pan, soak in cold water sprinkled with baking soda and let stand several hours. Then wash as usual.

Sweet Muffins

Apple Bran

Good – Sweet

Makes: 8 large or 12 medium
Preheat oven to 400°F (200°C) and prepare pan.

In large bowl add and combine well:

Eggs	2
Light molasses	¼ cup (50 mL)
Honey	¼ cup (50 mL)
Oil	½ cup (125 mL)
All-Bran cereal	1 cup (250 mL)
Chopped apple	1½ cups (375 mL), lightly packed
Raisins	¼ cup (50 mL)

In smaller bowl combine well:

All-purpose flour	1 cup (250 mL), unsifted
Baking soda	2 tsp. (10 mL)
Cinnamon	½ tsp. (2 mL)
Nutmeg	¼ tsp. (1 mL)
Chopped walnuts	¼ cup (50 mL)

Combine wet and dry mixtures and fold together gently until just mixed. Spoon into prepared pan. Bake at 400°F (200°C) for 20 minutes. Remove from pan and cool on rack.

HINT

The apple flavour is more apparent when eaten cold.

SERVING SUGGESTION

Serve with unsalted butter and Cheddar for breakfast or lunch, or with cottage cheese and fruit.

Apple Carrot

Makes: 12 medium
Preheat oven to 375°F (190°C) and prepare pan.

In large bowl add and combine well:

Eggs	3
Sugar	⅔ cup (150 mL)
Oil	½ cup (125 mL)
Shredded apple	1 cup (250 mL), 1 medium
Shredded carrot	1 cup (250 mL), 1½ medium
Vanilla	1 tsp. (5 mL)

In smaller bowl combine well:

Graham flour	1 cup (250 mL), unsifted
Cake and pastry flour	1 cup (250 mL), unsifted
Baking powder	1 Tbsp. (15 mL)
Baking soda	½ tsp. (2 mL)
Salt	½ tsp. (2 mL)
Cinnamon	½ tsp. (2 mL)
Chopped walnuts or pecans	½ cup (125 mL), optional

Combine wet and dry mixtures and fold together gently until just mixed. Spoon into prepared pan and decorate top of each muffin with a walnut or pecan half. Bake at 375°F (190°C) for 25 to 30 minutes. Remove from pan and cool on rack.

HINT

Toss grated apple in lemon juice to prevent darkening.

SERVING SUGGESTION

Make *Cinnamon Crumble Topping* — Mix 4 Tbsp. (50 mL) sugar, 2 Tbsp. (30 mL) flour, ½ tsp. (2 mL) cinnamon and 1 Tbsp. (15 mL) softened butter. Mix well by rubbing together with fingers. Sprinkle on muffin tops before baking.

Apple Cinnamon

Makes: 12 medium
Preheat oven to 400°F (200°C) and prepare pan.

In large bowl add and combine well:

Eggs	2
Brown sugar	½ cup (125 mL)
Oil	½ cup (125 mL)
Apple juice	½ cup (125 mL)
Chopped apple	2 cups (500 mL), 2 medium
Raisins	¼ cup (50 mL)
Vanilla	1 tsp. (5 mL)

In smaller bowl combine well:

Whole-wheat flour	1 cup (250 mL), unsifted
Cake and pastry flour	1 cup (250 mL), unsifted
Baking powder	1 Tbsp. (15 mL)
Baking soda	½ tsp. (2 mL)
Salt	½ tsp. (2 mL)
Cinnamon	1 tsp. (5 mL)
Chopped walnuts	½ cup (125 mL), optional

Combine wet and dry mixtures and fold together until just mixed. Spoon into prepared pan. Bake at 400°F (200°C) for 20 to 25 minutes. Remove from pan and cool on rack.

VARIATION

Apple Ginger — Omit cinnamon and raisins. Add 8 pieces finely chopped ginger (or to taste) and toss into dry mixture.

SERVING SUGGESTION

Make *Cinnamon Sugar Topping* — Mix ½ cup (125 mL) granulated sugar with 1 Tbsp. (15 mL) cinnamon. Melt ¼ cup (50 mL) butter and dip hot muffins in melted butter, then cinnamon sugar. Serve. Store leftover cinnamon sugar in a covered jar.

Apple Oatmeal

Good but not sweet add 1 T. Bn. Sugar

Makes: 10 large or 14 medium
Preheat oven to 400°F (200°C) and prepare pan.

In large bowl add and combine well:

Eggs	2
Honey	3 Tbsp. (45 mL)
Oil	½ cup (125 mL)
Milk	1 cup (250 mL)
Regular rolled oats (oatmeal)	1 cup (250 mL)
Chopped apple	2 cups (500 mL), 2 medium
Raisins	½ cup (125 mL)
Vanilla	1 tsp. (5 mL)

In smaller bowl combine well:

All-purpose flour	2 cups (500 mL), unsifted
Baking powder	1 Tbsp. (15 mL)
Baking soda	½ tsp. (2 mL)
Salt	½ tsp. (2 mL)
Cinnamon	1 tsp. (5 mL)

Combine wet and dry mixtures and fold together gently until just mixed. Bake at 400°F (200°C) for 20 to 25 minutes. Remove from pan and cool on rack.

VARIATION

Apple Wheat — Substitute wheat flakes for rolled oats.

HINT

For true oatmeal flavour, use regular rolled oats. Quick-cooking, not instant, oatmeal may be substituted, but the pleasant chewiness will be lost.

Apple Plus

Preheat oven to 400°F (200°C) and prepare pan.

In a large bowl add and combine well:

Eggs	2
Honey	¼ cup (50 mL)
Light molasses	¼ cup (50 mL)
Oil	½ cup (125 mL)
Apple juice	¾ cup (175 mL)
Finely chopped apple	1 cup (250 mL), 1 medium
Currants or raisins	½ cup (125 mL)

In smaller bowl combine well:

All-purpose flour	1 cup (250 mL), unsifted
Whole-wheat flour	½ cup (125 mL), unsifted
Raw wheat germ	¼ cup (50 mL)
Baking powder	1 Tbsp. (15 mL)
Baking soda	1 tsp. (5 mL)
Salt	¼ tsp. (1 mL)
Nutmeg	¼ tsp. (1 mL)
Chopped walnuts or pecans	½ cup (125 mL)

Combine wet and dry mixtures and fold together gently until just mixed. Spoon into prepared pan. Bake at 400°F (200°C) for 25 minutes. Remove from pan and cool on rack.

HINT

Molasses will pour out of a measuring cup easily if you measure oil in the same cup first.

SERVING SUGGESTION

Serve with *Cinnamon Topping* (see *Apple Cinnamon* muffin), or make *Cinnamon Butter* by creaming ½ cup (125 mL) unsalted butter together with ¼ cup (50 mL) cinnamon sugar and beating until light and fluffy.

Applesauce Spice Raisin

Makes: 12 medium
Preheat oven to 400°F (200°C) and prepare pan.

In large bowl add and combine well:

Eggs	2
Brown sugar	⅓ cup (75 mL)
Oil	½ cup (125 mL)
Applesauce	1 cup (250 mL), canned
Raisins	½ cup (125 mL)

In smaller bowl combine well:

All-purpose flour	1¾ cup (425 mL), unsifted
Baking powder	1 tsp. (5 mL)
Baking soda	1 tsp. (5 mL)
Salt	¼ tsp. (1 mL)
Cinnamon	½ tsp. (2 mL)
Nutmeg	½ tsp. (2 mL)
Allspice	⅛ tsp. (0.5 mL)

Combine wet and dry mixtures and fold together gently until just mixed. Spoon into prepared pan. Bake at 400°F (200°C) for 20 to 25 minutes. Remove from pan and cool on rack.

VARIATION

Whole-Wheat or Graham Applesauce — Substitute 1 cup (250 mL) unsifted whole-wheat or graham flour plus ¾ cup (175 mL) unsifted cake and pastry flour for 1¾ cup (425 mL) all-purpose flour.

HINT

To substitute homemade applesauce for canned, adjust spices and consistency to that of canned.

Apricot

Makes: 10 medium
Preheat oven to 400°F (200°C) and prepare pan.

Make apricot purée:

Bring ¼ lb. (125 gm) dried apricots plus ¾ cup (175 mL) water to a boil. Cover and simmer 10 to 15 minutes. Put mixture in a food processor or blender and reduce to a purée. (Don't worry if the purée is not totally smooth.) Set aside.

In large bowl add and combine well:

Eggs	2
Brown sugar	½ cup (125 mL)
Oil	¼ cup (50 mL)
Apricot purée	¾ cup (175 mL), prepared as above
Orange extract	1 tsp. (5 mL)

In smaller bowl combine well:

All-purpose flour	1½ cups (375 mL), unsifted
Baking powder	1 Tbsp. (15 mL)
Baking soda	½ tsp. (2 mL)
Salt	½ tsp. (2 mL)
Chopped walnuts or pecans	½ cup (125 mL), optional

Combine wet and dry mixtures and fold together gently until just mixed. Spoon into prepared pan and decorate top of each muffin with a piece of dried apricot or nut. Bake at 400°F (200°C) for 20 to 25 minutes. Remove from pan and cool on rack.

VARIATIONS

Prune — Make a prune purée. Prepare as apricot purée (above) substituting equal quantity of pitted dried prunes. Substitute 1 tsp. (5 mL) vanilla for orange extract.

Apricot or Prune Graham — Substitute 1 cup (250 mL) unsifted graham flour plus ½ cup (125 mL) unsifted cake and pastry flour for all-purpose flour. Add ½ cup (125 mL) plain yogurt to wet mixture.

Banana

Makes: 10 medium
Preheat oven to 375°F (190°C) and prepare pan.

In large bowl cream with electric mixer:

Butter	½ cup (125 mL)
Sugar	½ cup (125 mL)

Add and combine well:

Egg	1
Mashed banana	1 cup (250 mL), 2 medium
Baking soda	1 tsp. (5 mL) dissolved in 1 Tbsp. (15 mL) hot water

In smaller bowl combine well:

All-purpose flour	1½ cups (375 mL), unsifted
Salt	¼ tsp. (1 mL)
Nutmeg	1 tsp. (5 mL)
Chopped walnuts	½ cup (125 mL), optional

Combine wet and dry mixtures and fold together gently until just mixed. Spoon into prepared pan and decorate top of each muffin with a walnut half. Bake at 375°F (190°C) for 20 minutes. Remove from pan and cool on rack.

VARIATIONS

Banana Prune — Add 1 cup (250 mL) chopped pitted prunes to the batter.
Banana Carob — Reduce sugar to ⅓ cup (75 mL) and add ¼ cup (50 mL) carob powder to dry mixture. Omit nutmeg and add 1 tsp. (5 mL) vanilla to wet mixture.
Banana Chocolate Chip or Carob Chip — Add ½ cup (125 mL) chocolate or carob chips to batter.

Banana Carrot

Makes: 12 medium
Preheat oven to 400°F (200°C) and prepare pan.

In large bowl add and combine well:

Eggs	2
Brown sugar	½ cup (125 mL)
Oil	½ cup (125 mL)
Buttermilk	½ cup (125 mL)
Grated carrot	1 cup (250 mL), 1 large
Mashed banana	½ cup (125 mL), 1 medium
Vanilla	1 tsp. (5 mL)
Raisins	¼ cup (50 mL), optional

In smaller bowl combine well:

All-purpose flour	1½ cups (375 mL), unsifted
Baking powder	2 tsp. (10 mL)
Baking soda	1 tsp. (5 mL)
Salt	¼ tsp. (1 mL)
Nutmeg	½ tsp. (2 mL)
Ground cloves	one pinch

Combine wet and dry mixtures and fold together gently until just mixed. Spoon into prepared pan. Bake at 400°F (200°C) for 20 minutes. Remove from pan and cool on rack.

HINT

For very young children omit raisins and nuts.

SERVING SUGGESTION

A good muffin for youngsters.

Banana Coconut

Makes: 24 miniature or 12 medium
Preheat oven to 375°F (190°C) and prepare pan.

In large bowl add and combine well:

Egg	1
Sugar	½ cup (125 mL)
Butter or margarine	½ cup (125 mL), melted
Buttermilk or plain yogurt	½ cup (125 mL)
Mashed banana	½ cup (125 mL), 1 medium
Vanilla	1 tsp. (5 mL)
Sweetened flaked or shredded coconut	1 cup (250 mL)

In smaller bowl combine well:

All-purpose flour	1½ cups (375 mL), unsifted
Baking powder	1½ tsp. (7 mL)
Baking soda	1 tsp. (5 mL)
Salt	¼ tsp. (1 mL)
Nutmeg	½ tsp. (2 mL)
Ground cloves	one pinch

Combine wet and dry mixtures and fold together gently until just mixed. Spoon into prepared pan. Bake at 375°F (190°C) for 20 to 25 minutes. Remove from pan and cool on rack.

VARIATION

Unsweetened desiccated coconut may be substituted; however, increase buttermilk or plain yogurt to ¾ cup (175 mL).

HINT

Do not bake with soft margarine.

SERVING SUGGESTION

Make in miniature pan and serve with lemon tea.

Banana Orange

250 cal. for 10 muffin

Makes: 12 medium
Preheat oven to 400°F (200°C) and prepare pan.

In a food processor or blender reduce to a purée:

Orange	1 whole, including skin

In large bowl add and combine well:

Eggs	2
Brown sugar	½ cup (125 mL)
Oil	½ cup (125 mL)
Mashed banana	2 small
Orange purée	as prepared above
Orange juice	½ cup (125 mL)

In smaller bowl combine well:

All-purpose flour	1½ cups (375 mL), unsifted
Baking powder	1 Tbsp. (15 mL)
Baking soda	½ tsp. (2 mL)
Salt	½ tsp. (2 mL)
Nutmeg	¼ tsp. (1 mL)
Chopped walnuts	1 cup (250 mL), optional

Combine wet and dry mixtures and fold together gently until just mixed. Spoon into prepared pan. Bake at 400°F (200°C) for 20 to 25 minutes. Remove from pan and cool on rack.

HINT

Orange purée and mashed banana together should measure 1 cup (250 mL). To grate orange rind with a food processor, see *Citrus* muffin.

Banana Peanut Butter

Makes: 10 medium
Preheat oven to 400°F (200°C) and prepare pan.

In large bowl add and combine well:

Eggs	2
Honey	½ cup (125 mL)
Oil	½ cup (125 mL)
Mashed banana	1 cup (250 mL), 2 medium
Peanut butter	½ cup (125 mL), smooth or crunchy
Vanilla	1 tsp. (5 mL)

In smaller bowl combine well:

All-purpose flour	1½ cups (375 mL), unsifted
Baking powder	1 Tbsp. (15 mL)
Baking soda	½ tsp. (2 mL)
Salt	½ tsp. (2 mL)

Combine wet and dry mixtures and fold together gently until just mixed. Spoon into prepared pan. Bake at 400°F (200°C) for 20 minutes. Remove from pan and cool on rack.

HINT

Make with creamy peanut butter for infants and youngsters.

Blueberry Bran Wheat Germ

Makes: 12 large or 16 medium
Preheat oven to 400°F (200°C) and prepare pan.

In large bowl add and combine well:

Eggs	3
Brown sugar	1 cup (250 mL)
Oil	½ cup (125 mL)
Buttermilk	2 cups (500 mL)
Vanilla	1 tsp. (15 mL)
Raw wheat germ	1 cup (250 mL)
Bran	1 cup (250 mL)

In smaller bowl combine well:

All-purpose flour	2 cups (500 mL), unsifted
Baking powder	2 tsp. (10 mL)
Baking soda	2 tsp. (10 mL)
Salt	½ tsp. (2 mL)
Fresh or frozen blueberries	1½ cups (375 mL), whole

Combine wet and dry mixtures and fold together gently until just mixed. Bake at 400°F (200°C) for 20 to 25 minutes. Remove from pan and cool on rack.

VARIATION

Cranberry Bran Wheat Germ — Substitute 1½ cups (375 mL) chopped fresh or frozen cranberries for blueberries.

HINT

Do not defrost frozen blueberries or cranberries before using. Defrosted berries produce a highly discoloured batter.

Buttermilk Bran

Makes: 36 medium
Preheat oven to 400°F (200°C) and prepare pans.

In large bowl add and combine well:

Eggs	6
Brown sugar	1 cup (250 mL)
Light molasses	½ cup (125 mL)
Oil	1½ cups (375 mL)
Vanilla	2 tsp. (10 mL)
Buttermilk	1 quart (1000 mL)
Bran	4½ cups (1125 mL)
Chopped prunes or dates	1 cup (250 mL)
Currants or raisins	1 cup (250 mL)

In smaller bowl combine well:

All-purpose flour	2 cups (500 mL), unsifted
Whole-wheat flour	2 cups (500 mL), unsifted
Baking powder	4 tsp. (20 mL)
Baking soda	4 tsp. (20 mL)
Chopped walnuts or pecans	1 cup (250 mL), optional

Combine wet and dry mixtures and fold together gently until just mixed. Spoon into prepared pans. Bake at 400°F (200°C) for 20 to 25 minutes. Remove from pans and cool on rack.

VARIATIONS

Buttermilk Bran Wheat Flake — Substitute 2½ cups (625 mL) bran plus 2 cups (500 mL) wheat flakes for 4½ cups (1125 mL) bran.
Buttermilk Bran Wheat Germ — Substitute 2½ cups (625 mL) bran and 2 cups (500 mL) wheat germ for 4½ cups (1125 mL) bran.
Buttermilk Bran Oatmeal — Substitute 2½ cups (625 mL) bran and 2 cups (500 mL) regular rolled oats for 4½ cups (1125 mL) bran.
Buttermilk Bran Graham — Substitute 2 cups (500 mL) unsifted graham flour for whole-wheat flour.

Buttermilk Oatmeal

Makes: 12 medium
Preheat oven to 400°F (200°C) and prepare pan.

Mix and allow to soak for 10 *minutes:*

Regular rolled oats (oatmeal)	1½ cups (375 mL)
Buttermilk	1½ cups (375 mL)

In large bowl add and combine well:

Eggs	2
Brown sugar	½ cup (125 mL)
Butter or margarine	½ cup (125 mL), melted
Rolled oats mixture	as prepared above
Vanilla	1 tsp. (5 mL)

(added 2 T. sugar needs more)

In smaller bowl combine well:

All-purpose flour	1½ cups (375 mL), unsifted
Baking powder	1 Tbsp. (15 mL)
Baking soda	½ tsp. (2 mL)
Salt	½ tsp. (2 mL)
Nutmeg	⅛ tsp. (0.5 mL)

Combine wet and dry mixtures and fold together gently until just mixed. Spoon into prepared pan. Bake at 400°F (200°C) for 20 minutes. Remove from pan and cool on rack.

VARIATIONS

Oatmeal Blueberry — Alter rolled oats mixture to measure 1 cup (250 mL) regular rolled oats soaked in 1 cup (250 mL) buttermilk. Substitute ½ cup (125 mL) graham flour plus 1 cup (250 mL) all-purpose flour for 1½ cups (375 mL) all-purpose flour. Add 1 cup (250 mL) fresh or frozen blueberries at the last moment.

Oatmeal Cranberry — Alter rolled oats mixture to measure 1 cup (250 mL) regular rolled oats soaked in 1 cup (250 mL) buttermilk. Increase brown sugar to ⅔ cup (150 mL). Add 1 cup (250 mL) chopped fresh or frozen cranberries at the last moment.

Butternut Squash

Makes: 12 medium
Preheat oven to 400°F (200°C) and prepare pan.

To prepare butternut squash purée:
Bake one butternut squash (1 lb. or 500 g) until very soft (approx. one hour). Sieve pulp, measure and reserve ¾ cup (175 mL). If you have a blender or food processor, remove seeds and purée pulp.

In large bowl add and combine well:

Eggs	2
Brown sugar	½ cup (125 mL)
Butter or margarine	½ cup (125 mL), melted
Milk	¾ cup (175 mL)
Butternut squash purée	¾ cup (175 mL), prepared as above
Raisins	½ cup (125 mL)

In smaller bowl combine well:

All-purpose flour	1 cup (250 mL), unsifted
Whole-wheat flour	½ cup (125 mL), unsifted
Cake and pastry flour	½ cup (125 mL), unsifted
Baking powder	1 Tbsp. (15 mL)
Baking soda	½ tsp. (2 mL)
Salt	½ tsp. (2 mL)
Cinnamon	½ tsp. (2 mL)
Nutmeg	½ tsp. (2 mL)
Chopped walnuts or pecans	½ cup (125 mL)

Combine wet and dry mixtures and fold together gently until just mixed. Spoon into prepared pan and decorate top of each muffin with a walnut or pecan half. Bake at 400°F (200°C) for 20 to 25 minutes. Remove from pan and cool on rack.

HINT

Fold ½ cup (125 mL) roasted seeds or nuts (pumpkin, sesame or peanuts, soya nuts, etc.) into batter and sprinkle additional seeds or nuts on each muffin top.

Frozen butternut squash may be substituted with good results.

Carob Orange

Makes: 14 medium
Preheat oven to 400°F (200°C) and prepare pan.

In a food processor or blender reduce to a purée:

Orange	1 whole, including skin

In large bowl add and combine well:

Eggs	2
Brown sugar	¼ cup (50 mL)
Honey	¼ cup (50 mL)
Orange purée	as prepared above
Oil	½ cup (125 mL)
Milk	1 cup (250 mL)
Vanilla	1 tsp. (5 mL)

In smaller bowl combine well:

All-purpose flour	2 cups (500 mL), unsifted
Carob powder	¼ cup (50 mL)
Baking powder	1 Tbsp. (15 mL)
Baking soda	½ tsp. (2 mL)
Ground ginger	¼ tsp. (1 mL)
Chopped walnuts or pecans	½ cup (125 mL)

Combine wet and dry mixtures and fold together gently until just mixed. Spoon into prepared pan. Bake at 400°F (200°C) for 20 minutes. Remove from pan and cool on rack.

VARIATIONS

Chocolate Orange — Increase brown sugar to ½ cup (125 mL). Substitute cocoa for carob powder.
Carob Chip — Omit puréed orange. Substitute ½ cup (125 mL) carob chips for nuts.

SERVING SUGGESTION

Serve with whipped cream cheese.

Cheddar

Makes: 10 medium
Preheat oven to 400°F (200°C) and prepare pan.

In large bowl add and combine well:

Eggs	2
Honey or maple syrup	¼ cup (50 mL)
Oil	¼ cup (50 mL)
Buttermilk or plain yogurt	½ cup (125 mL)
Grated old Cheddar cheese	1 cup (250 mL), ¼ lb.
Prepared mustard	1 tsp. (5 mL)

In smaller bowl combine well:

Cake and pastry flour	1 cup (250 mL), unsifted
Whole-wheat flour	½ cup (125 mL), unsifted
Baking powder	1½ tsp. (7 mL)
Baking soda	½ tsp. (2 mL)
Salt	½ tsp. (2 mL)

Combine wet and dry mixtures and fold together gently until just mixed. Spoon into prepared pan. Bake at 400°F (200°C) for 20 minutes. Remove from pan and cool on rack.

VARIATIONS

Bacon Cheddar — Omit salt. Add ½ cup (125 mL) fried, crisp, crumbled bacon to batter when combining wet and dry mixtures.

Apple Cheddar — Makes: 12 medium. Omit prepared mustard. For all-purpose flour substitute 1 cup (250 mL) unsifted cake and pastry flour plus ½ cup (125 mL) unsifted whole-wheat flour. Add 1 cup (250 mL) chopped apple, peeled to wet mixture.

Date Cheese — Makes: 12 medium. Omit prepared mustard. Add ¾ cup (175 mL) chopped dates to wet mixture.

Buttery Carrot — Makes: 12 medium. Substitute ¾ cup (175 mL) mild Cheddar (not medium) for old cheese. Add 1 cup (250 mL) grated carrot to wet mixture. Substitute 1½ cups (375 mL) unsifted all-purpose flour for whole-wheat/cake and pastry flour mixture.

Cherry Almond or Pecan

Makes: 12 medium
Preheat oven to 400°F (200°C) and prepare pan.

In large bowl add and combine well:

Eggs	4
Sugar	½ cup (125 mL)
Butter or margarine	½ cup (125 mL), melted
Whole pitted sour cherries	1 cup (250 mL), (1 14-oz. or 398-mL can, drained)
Almond extract	½ tsp. (2 mL)

In smaller bowl combine well:

All-purpose flour	2 cups (500 mL), unsifted
Baking powder	1 Tbsp. (15 mL)
Baking soda	1 tsp. (5 mL)
Salt	¼ tsp. (1 mL)
Finely chopped almonds or pecans	1 cup (250 mL)

Combine wet and dry mixtures and fold together gently until just mixed. Spoon into prepared pan. Bake at 400°F (200°C) for 20 minutes. Remove from pan and cool on rack.

VARIATIONS

Fruit Cocktail — Substitute 1 cup (250 mL) well-drained fruit cocktail (1 14-oz. or 398-mL can) for sour red cherries. Omit nuts.

HINT

The *Cherry Almond* or *Pecan* muffin looks and tastes its best when canned pitted cherries are left whole and nuts are finely chopped.

SERVING SUGGESTION

Make the *Fruit Cocktail* muffin for children and decorate the top of each muffin with a maraschino cherry half.

Cherry Pineapple

Makes: 24 miniature or 12 medium
Preheat oven to 400°F (200°C) and prepare pan.

In large bowl add and combine well:

Eggs	2
Sugar	⅓ cup (75 mL)
Butter or margarine	¼ cup (50 mL), melted
Maraschino cherry juice	¼ cup (50 mL)
Unsweetened crushed pineapple	1 cup (250 mL), undrained
Coarsely chopped maraschino cherries	¼ cup (50 mL), approx. 18
Almond extract	½ tsp. (2 mL)

In smaller bowl combine well:

All-purpose flour	2 cups (500 mL), unsifted
Baking powder	1 Tbsp. (15 mL)
Baking soda	½ tsp. (2 mL)
Salt	½ tsp. (2 mL)

Combine wet and dry mixtures and fold together gently until just mixed. Spoon into prepared pan and decorate top with a maraschino cherry half. Bake at 400°F (200°C) for 15 to 20 minutes. Remove from pan and cool on rack.

HINT

Maraschino cherries, as well as candied or dried fruits, are chopped easily with kitchen shears.

SERVING SUGGESTION

A pretty muffin that needs no butter. Make in miniature pan for a party or tea-time sweet. Decorate the top of each muffin with a maraschino cherry half.

Chocolate Chocolate Chip

Makes: 10 medium
Preheat oven to 400°F (200°C) and prepare pan.

In *large bowl add and combine well*:

Eggs	2
Oil	½ cup (125 mL)
Milk	1 cup (250 mL)
Vanilla	1 tsp. (5 mL)

In *smaller bowl combine well*:

All-purpose flour	1¾ cups (425 mL), unsifted
Sugar	½ cup (125 mL)
Pure cocoa	¼ cup (50 mL)
Baking powder	1 Tbsp. (15 mL)
Salt	½ tsp. (2 mL)
Semi-sweet chocolate chips	½ cup (125 mL)

Combine wet and dry mixtures and fold together gently until just mixed. Spoon into prepared pan. Bake at 400°F (200°C) for 20 minutes. Remove from pan and cool on rack.

VARIATIONS

Maple Butterscotch Chip — Substitute light brown sugar for granulated. Omit cocoa and adjust all-purpose flour to 2 cups (500 mL) unsifted. Substitute 1 tsp. (5 mL) maple extract for vanilla and butterscotch chips for chocolate chips.

Chocolate Peanut Butter Chip — Substitute peanut butter chips for chocolate chips.

HINT

For an even richer chocolate flavour, use 2 Tbsp. (30 mL) semi-sweet liquid baking chocolate (available in a tube) and increase all-purpose flour to 2 cups (500 mL). Sprinkle extra chocolate chips on top of each muffin before baking.

Citrus (Lemon Orange)

Makes: 24 miniature or 12 medium
Preheat oven to 400°F (200°C) and prepare pan.

In large bowl add and combine well:

Eggs	2
Sugar	½ cup (125 mL)
Oil	½ cup (125 mL)
Milk	½ cup (125 mL)
Grated rind of 1 lemon	approx. 1 Tbsp. (15 mL)
Grated rind of 1 orange	approx. 1½ Tbsp. (22 mL)
Juice of 1 lemon	lemon and orange juice should
Juice of 1 orange	measure ½ cup (125 mL) together

In smaller bowl combine well:

Cake and pastry flour	1¼ cups (300 mL), unsifted
Whole-wheat flour	1 cup (250 mL), unsifted
Baking powder	1 Tbsp. (15 mL)
Baking soda	½ tsp. (2 mL)
Salt	½ tsp. (2 mL)

Combine wet and dry mixtures and fold together gently until just mixed. Spoon into prepared pan. Bake at 400°F (200°C) for 20 minutes. Remove from pan and cool on rack.

HINT

To grate citrus peel with a food processor, remove the peel, chop into 1″ pieces and process together with ¼ cup (50 mL) or ½ cup (125 mL) of sugar. Calculate sugar into the recipe. Try not to remove any of the bitter white membrane underneath the peel. If the fruit is thick skinned and firm, peel can be removed easily with a vegetable peeler.

SERVING SUGGESTION

Very good plain with lemon tea, or serve with *Orange Butter*. Make *Orange Butter* — Grate the peel of 2 oranges (approx. 3 Tbsp.) (45 mL) and mix well with ½ cup (125 mL) granulated sugar. Add to 1 cup (250 mL) unsalted butter, and beat until light and fluffy. If desired, freeze half.

Citrus Zucchini/Courgette

Makes: 24 miniature or 12 medium
Preheat oven to 400°F (200°C) and prepare pan.

In large bowl add and combine well:

Eggs	2
Sugar	⅔ cup (150 mL)
Oil	½ cup (125 mL)
Grated rind of 1 lemon	approx. 1 Tbsp. (15 mL)
Juice of 1 lemon	approx. ¼ cup (50 mL)
Grated zucchini/courgette	1½ cups (375 mL), unpeeled, approx. two small

In smaller bowl combine well:

All-purpose flour	2 cups (500 mL), unsifted
Baking powder	2 tsp. (10 mL)
Baking soda	½ tsp. (2 mL)
Salt	¼ tsp. (1 mL)
Nutmeg	⅛ tsp. (0.5 mL)

Combine wet and dry mixtures and fold together gently until just mixed. Spoon into prepared pan. Bake at 400°F (200°C) for 20 to 25 minutes. Remove from pan and cool on rack.

SERVING SUGGESTION

Make miniatures, hollow out slightly and fill with lemon curd. Serve larger muffins with *Lemon Cream Cheese Spread.* First make *Lemon Butter* (see *Cranberry Nut* muffin) and mix equal quantities of cream cheese and *Lemon Butter* and beat until light and fluffy.

Coconut

Makes: 26 miniature or 14 medium
Preheat oven to 400°F (200°C) and prepare pan.

In large bowl add and combine well:

Eggs	2
Sugar	½ cup (125 mL)
Butter or margarine	½ cup (125 mL), melted
Milk	¾ cup (175 mL)
Grated lemon rind	2 tsp. (10 mL)
Flaked sweetened coconut	1½ cups (375 mL)

In smaller bowl combine well:

Cake and pastry flour	1½ cups (375 mL), unsifted
Baking powder	1½ tsp. (7 mL)
Baking soda	½ tsp. (2 mL)
Salt	¼ tsp. (1 mL)

Combine wet and dry mixtures and fold together gently until just mixed. Spoon into prepared pan. Bake at 400°F (200°C) for 20 to 25 minutes. Remove from pan and cool on rack.

VARIATIONS

Chocolate Coconut — Add 3 Tbsp. (50 mL) cocoa plus an additional ¼ cup (50 mL) sugar to dry mixture.
Carob Coconut — Add 3 Tbsp. (50 mL) carob powder to dry mixture.
Chocolate Chip Coconut — Add ½ cup (125 mL) semi-sweet chocolate chips to coconut or chocolate coconut muffin batter.

Corn Wheat Germ

Makes: 15 medium or 12 large
Preheat oven to 400°F (200°C) and prepare pan.

Mix and allow to soak for 10 minutes:

Cornmeal	1 cup (250 mL)
Buttermilk	2 cups (500 mL)

In large bowl add and combine well:

Eggs	2
Sugar	½ cup (125 mL)
Oil	½ cup (125 mL)
Cornmeal mixture	as prepared above

In smaller bowl combine well:

All-purpose flour	1¾ cups (425 mL), unsifted
Raw wheat germ	1 cup (250 mL)
Baking powder	2 tsp. (10 mL)
Baking soda	1 tsp. (5 mL)
Salt	1 tsp. (5 mL)

Combine wet and dry mixtures and fold together gently until just mixed. Spoon into prepared pan. Bake at 400°F (200°C) for 20 minutes. Remove from pan and cool on rack.

VARIATION

Cornmeal with Preserves — Spoon 1 tsp. (5 mL) preserves on top of each muffin before baking (see *Peach Puffins*).

SERVING SUGGESTION

Excellent breakfast muffin with ham and eggs.

Cranberry Nut

Makes: 12 medium
Preheat oven to 400°F (200°C) and prepare pan.

In large bowl add and combine well:

Eggs	2
Butter or margarine	¼ cup (50 mL), melted
Milk	1 cup (250 mL)
Vanilla	1 tsp. (5 mL)

In smaller bowl combine well:

All-purpose flour	2 cups (500 mL), unsifted
Sugar	¾ cup (175 mL)
Baking powder	1 Tbsp. (15 mL)
Baking soda	½ tsp. (2 mL)
Salt	½ tsp. (2 mL)
Chopped fresh or frozen cranberries	1½ cups (375 mL)
Chopped walnuts	½ cup (125 mL), optional

Combine wet and dry mixtures and fold together gently until just mixed. Spoon into prepared pan. Bake at 400°F (200°C) for 25 minutes. Remove from pan and cool on rack.

VARIATION

Blueberry Nut — Substitute whole fresh or frozen blueberries for cranberries. Substitute 1 tsp. (5 mL) grated lemon rind for vanilla.

HINT

Do not defrost frozen blueberries or cranberries before using. Defrosted berries produce a highly discoloured batter.

SERVING SUGGESTION

Blueberry Nut goes especially well with Lemon Butter. Make Lemon Butter — Grate the rind of 3 lemons (approx. 3 Tbsp.) (45 mL) and mix well with ½ cup (125 mL) granulated sugar. Add to 1 cup (250 mL) unsalted butter and beat until light and fluffy.

Cream of Wheat

Makes: 12 medium
Preheat oven to 400°F (200°C) and prepare pan.

In large bowl add and combine well:

Eggs	2
Butter or margarine	½ cup (125 mL), melted
Milk	1 cup (250 mL)
Vanilla	1 tsp. (5 mL)

In smaller bowl combine well:

All-purpose flour	1¼ cups (300 mL), unsifted
Cream of Wheat	¾ cup (175 mL)
Sugar	½ cup (125 mL)
Baking powder	1 Tbsp. (15 mL)
Salt	½ tsp. (2 mL)

Combine wet and dry mixtures and fold together gently until just mixed. Spoon into prepared pan. Bake at 400°F (200°C) for 20 minutes. Remove from pan and cool on rack.

VARIATION

Durum Semolina or Farina — Substitute semolina or farina for Cream of Wheat.

SERVING SUGGESTIONS

For young children, place 1 tsp. (5 mL) jam on top of each muffin. With the back of a spoon, gently press half of the jam into the muffin. Bake and cool well. Do not use jelly; it will melt and run onto the pan.

This muffin is also good with an *Apple-Cinnamon* topping (see *Rice* muffin).

Crunchy Peanut Butter and Honey

Makes: 14 medium
Preheat oven to 375°F (190°C) and prepare pan.

In large bowl add and combine well:

Eggs	2
Honey	½ cup (125 mL)
Oil	¼ cup (50 mL)
Buttermilk	1 cup (250 mL)
Freshly ground peanut butter	1 cup (250 mL)
Vanilla	1 tsp. (5 mL)

In smaller bowl combine well:

Whole-wheat flour	1 cup (250 mL), unsifted
Cake and pastry flour	1 cup (250 mL), unsifted
Baking powder	2 tsp. (10 mL)
Baking soda	1 tsp. (5 mL)
Salt	½ tsp. (2 mL)
Chopped peanuts	½ cup (125 mL), unsalted raw

Combine wet and dry mixtures and fold together gently until just mixed. Spoon into prepared pan and sprinkle top of each muffin with chopped peanuts. Bake at 375°F (190°C) for 25 minutes. Remove from pan and cool on rack.

VARIATION

Omit salt and substitute ½ cup (125 mL) roasted pumpkin seeds for chopped peanuts. Sprinkle additional pumpkin seeds on each muffin top before baking.

HINT

To liquify honey that has crystallized, place honey pot or jar in hot water. Do not bake with hardened creamed honey.

Flaxseed

Makes: 12 medium
Preheat oven to 400°F (200°C) and prepare pan.

In large bowl add and combine well:

Eggs	2
Honey	¼ cup (50 mL)
Brown sugar	¼ cup (50 mL)
Oil	½ cup (125 mL)
Buttermilk	1 cup (250 mL)
Vanilla	1 tsp. (5 mL)

In smaller bowl combine well:

All-purpose flour	1 cup (250 mL), unsifted
Ground flaxseed	1 cup (250 mL)
Baking powder	1 tsp. (5 mL)
Baking soda	1 tsp. (5 mL)
Salt	¼ tsp. (1 mL)
Cinnamon	1 tsp. (5 mL)
Chopped walnuts or pecans	½ cup (125 mL)

Combine wet and dry mixtures and fold together gently until just mixed. Spoon into prepared pan and decorate top of each muffin with a walnut or pecan half. Bake at 400°F (200°C) for 20 minutes. Remove from pan and cool on rack.

HINT

An effective alternative to bran or prune. Grind flaxseeds in a coffee grinder if a nut grinder is not available.

flourless Bran

Makes: 8 medium
Preheat oven to 375°F (190°C) and prepare pan.

In large bowl add and combine well:

Eggs	2
Honey	2 Tbsp. (30 mL)
Light molasses	2 Tbsp. (30 mL)
Oil	¼ cup (50 mL)
Buttermilk	1 cup (250 mL)
Chopped dates or raisins	½ cup (125 mL)

In smaller bowl combine well:

Bran	1½ cups (375 mL)
Raw wheat germ	1 cup (250 mL)
Baking powder	1½ tsp. (7 mL)
Baking soda	1 tsp. (5 mL)
Chopped walnuts or pecans or sunflower seeds	½ cup (125 mL)

Combine wet and dry mixtures and fold together gently until just mixed. Spoon into prepared pan. Bake at 375°F (190°C) for 15 to 20 minutes. Remove from pan and cool on rack.

HINT

When chopping dried fruit, avoid stickiness by tossing fruit in a small amount of flour first, then calculate the flour into your recipe. If you have a food processor, add the dried fruit plus ¼ or ½ cup flour (50 or 125 mL) to processor bowl and chop.

Ginger Nut

Makes: 12 medium
Preheat oven to 400°F (200°C) and prepare pan.

In large bowl add and combine well:

Eggs	2
Brown sugar	½ cup (125 mL)
Oil	½ cup (125 mL)
Plain yogurt or buttermilk	1 cup (250 mL)

In smaller bowl combine well:

Whole-wheat flour	1 cup (250 mL), unsifted
Cake and pastry flour	1 cup (250 mL), unsifted
Finely chopped crystallized ginger	8 pieces
Baking powder	1 tsp. (5 mL)
Baking soda	1 tsp. (5 mL)
Chopped pecans or walnuts	½ cup (125 mL)

Combine wet and dry mixtures and fold together gently until just mixed. Spoon into prepared pan and decorate top of each muffin with a walnut or pecan half. Bake at 400°F (200°C) for 20 to 25 minutes. Remove from pan and cool on rack.

VARIATION

Chocolate Ginger Nut — Substitute 2 cups (500 mL) unsifted all-purpose flour for whole-wheat and cake and pastry flour. In blender or food processor, chop ½ cup (125 mL) semi-sweet chocolate chips into smaller chips and add to dry mixture.

Granola

Makes: 10 large or 14 medium
Preheat oven to 400°F (200°C) and prepare pan.

In large bowl add and combine well:

Eggs	2
Brown sugar	¼ cup (50 mL)
Oil	½ cup (125 mL)
Buttermilk	1 cup (250 mL)
Vanilla	1 tsp. (5 mL)

In smaller bowl combine well:

Granola	2 cups (500 mL)
All-purpose flour	1 cup (250 mL), unsifted
Baking powder	2 tsp. (10 mL)
Baking soda	½ tsp. (2 mL)
Salt	½ tsp. (2 mL)

Combine wet and dry mixtures and fold together gently until just mixed. Spoon into prepared pan and sprinkle each muffin top with granola. Bake at 400°F (200°C) for 15 to 20 minutes. Remove from pan and cool on rack.

HINT

Best results are achieved when the granola is not overly sweet and separates easily.

Jam Puffins

good with 2 T. butter oil balance + 2 T. maple syrup

Makes: 12 medium
Preheat oven to 400°F (200°C) and prepare pan.

In large bowl add and combine well:

Eggs	2
Brown sugar	½ cup (125 mL)
Butter or margarine	½ cup (125 mL), melted
Buttermilk	1¼ cups (300 mL)
Maple extract	1 tsp. (5 mL)

In smaller bowl combine well:

Whole-wheat flour	1 cup (250 mL), unsifted
Cake and pastry flour	1 cup (250 mL), unsifted
Baking powder	1 tsp. (5 mL)
Baking soda	1 tsp. (5 mL)
Salt	½ tsp. (2 mL)

Topping:

Peach jam	12 tsp. (60 mL)

Combine wet and dry mixtures and fold together gently until just mixed. Spoon into prepared pan (fill only ⅔ full). Place 1 tsp. (5 mL) peach jam on each muffin top and press jam gently with spoon. Bake at 400°F (200°C) for 20 minutes. Remove from pan and cool on rack.

VARIATION

Red Jam Puffins — Substitute strawberry or raspberry jam for peach jam. Substitute 1 tsp. (5 mL) vanilla for maple extract.

Maple Graham

Makes: 10 medium
Preheat oven to 400°F (200°C) and prepare pan.

In *large bowl add and combine well*:

Eggs	2
Maple syrup	½ cup (125 mL)
Oil	½ cup (125 mL)
Buttermilk	¾ cup (175 mL)
Maple extract	½ tsp. (2 mL)

In *smaller bowl combine well*:

Graham flour	1 cup (250 mL), unsifted
Cake and pastry flour	½ cup (125 mL), unsifted
Baking powder	1½ tsp. (7 mL)
Baking soda	½ tsp. (2 mL)
Salt	½ tsp. (2 mL)
Chopped pecans	½ cup (125 mL)

Combine wet and dry mixtures and fold together gently until just mixed. Spoon into prepared pan and decorate top of each muffin with a pecan half. Bake at 400°F (200°C) for 20 minutes. Remove from pan and cool on rack.

VARIATION

Whole-Wheat Maple Nut — Substitute 1 cup (250 mL) unsifted whole-wheat flour for graham flour. Substitute 1 cup (250 mL) chopped walnuts for ½ cup (125 mL) chopped pecans.

SERVING SUGGESTION

Good warm with marmalade or *Cinnamon Butter* (see *Apple Plus* muffin).

Mocha Almond

Makes: 20 miniature or 10 medium
Preheat oven to 400°F (200°C) and prepare pan.

In *large bowl add and combine well*:

Instant coffee	2 tsp. (10 mL) dissolved in 1 Tbsp. (15 mL) hot water
Egg	1
Oil	¼ cup (50 mL)
Milk	1 cup (250 mL)
Orange or vanilla extract	1 tsp. (5 mL)

In *smaller bowl combine well*:

All-purpose flour	1½ cups (375 mL), unsifted
Sugar	½ cup (125 mL)
Pure cocoa	2 Tbsp. (30 mL)
Baking powder	1 tsp. (5 mL)
Baking soda	½ tsp. (2 mL)
Salt	¼ tsp. (1 mL)
Chopped or sliced almonds	½ cup (125 mL)

Combine wet and dry mixtures and fold together gently until just mixed. Spoon into prepared pan and decorate top of each muffin with chopped or sliced almonds. Bake at 400°F (200°C) for 25 minutes. Remove from pan and cool on rack.

HINT

For an even richer chocolate flavour use 2 Tbsp. (30 mL) semi-sweet liquid baking chocolate (available in a tube) and increase flour to 1¾ cups (425 mL).

SERVING SUGGESTION

Make in miniature and serve after dinner with coffee.

Oatmeal Coconut

Makes: 14 medium
Preheat oven to 400°F (200°C) and prepare pan.

Combine and allow to cool:

Regular rolled oats (oatmeal)	1 cup (250 mL)
Boiling water	1 cup (250 mL) *Pineapple juice*
Butter or margarine	½ cup (125 mL)

In large bowl add and combine well:

Eggs	2
Brown sugar	¾ cup (175 mL)
Rolled oats mixture	as prepared above
Vanilla	1 tsp. (5 mL)

In smaller bowl combine well:

All-purpose flour	1 cup (250 mL), unsifted
Raw wheat germ	½ cup (125 mL)
Unsweetened desiccated coconut	1 cup (250 mL)
Baking powder	1 Tbsp. (15 mL)
Baking soda	½ tsp. (2 mL)
Salt	½ tsp. (2 mL)

Combine wet and dry mixtures and fold together gently until just mixed. Spoon into prepared pan. Bake at 400°F (200°C) for 20 to 25 minutes. Remove from pan and cool on rack.

HINT

Sweetened flaked or shredded coconut may be substituted, but decrease sugar to ½ cup (125 mL) and increase unsifted all-purpose flour to 1¼ cups (300 mL).

Oatmeal Pineapple

Makes: 12 medium
Preheat oven to 400°F (200°C) and prepare pan.

In large bowl add and combine well:

Eggs	2
Brown sugar	½ cup (125 mL)
Oil	½ cup (125 mL)
Milk or orange juice	¼ cup (50 mL)
Crushed unsweetened pineapple	1 cup (250 mL), undrained
Regular rolled oats (oatmeal)	1 cup (250 mL)
Grated orange rind	1 tsp. (5 mL)

In smaller bowl combine well:

All-purpose flour	1½ cups (375 mL), unsifted
Baking powder	1 Tbsp. (15 mL)
Baking soda	½ tsp. (2 mL)
Salt	½ tsp. (2 mL)

Combine wet and dry mixtures and fold together gently until just mixed. Spoon into prepared pan. Bake at 400°F (200°C) for 20 to 25 minutes. Remove from pan and cool on rack.

VARIATION

Oatmeal Apple — Substitute 1 cup (250 mL) grated apple for crushed pineapple. Add ½ cup (125 mL) raisins.

HINT

This muffin is best when fully cooled. Freezes well.

Oatmeal Prune

Makes: 12 large or 15 medium
Preheat oven to 400°F (200°C) and prepare pan.

In large bowl add and combine well:

Eggs	2
Oil	¼ cup (50 mL)
Milk	1 cup (250 mL)
Vanilla	1 tsp. (5 mL)
Chopped prunes	1 cup (250 mL), pitted

In smaller bowl combine well:

Cake and pastry flour	2 cups (500 mL), unsifted
Regular rolled oats (oatmeal)	1 cup (250 mL)
Sugar	¾ cup (175 mL)
Baking powder	1 Tbsp. (15 mL)
Salt	¾ tsp. (3 mL)

Combine wet and dry mixtures and fold together gently until just mixed. Spoon into prepared pan. Bake at 400°F (200°C) for 15 minutes. Remove from pan and cool on rack.

VARIATION

Oatmeal Fig — Substitute ½ cup (125 mL) chopped dried black mission figs for prunes. Add ½ cup (125 mL) chopped walnuts or pecans.

HINT

This batter is stark white and very thick. The baked muffin is very light in colour.

Orange

Makes: 12 medium
Preheat oven to 400°F (200°C) and prepare pan.

In a food processor or blender reduce to a purée:

Orange	1 whole, including skin

In large bowl add and combine well:

Egg	1
Brown sugar	½ cup (125 mL)
Orange purée	as prepared above
Oil	½ cup (125 mL)
Orange juice	½ cup (125 mL)
Chopped black mission figs	¼ cup (50 mL)
Chopped dates	¼ cup (50 mL)

In smaller bowl combine well:

All-purpose flour	½ cup (125 mL), unsifted
Wheat germ	½ cup (125 mL)
Bran	½ cup (125 mL)
Baking powder	1 tsp. (5 mL)
Baking soda	1 tsp. (5 mL)
Salt	¼ tsp. (1 mL)

Combine wet and dry mixtures and fold together gently until just mixed. Spoon into prepared pan. Bake at 400°F (200°C) for 15 to 20 minutes. Remove from pan and cool on rack.

Orange French Breakfast

Makes: 8 medium
Preheat oven to 375°F (190°C) and prepare pan.

In large bowl cream with electric mixer:

Shortening	¼ cup (50 mL)
Butter	2 Tbsp. (30 mL)
Sugar	½ cup (125 mL)
Eggs	2
Grated rind of 1 orange	approx. 1½ Tbsp. (22 mL)

In smaller bowl combine well:

Cake and pastry flour	1½ cups (375 mL), unsifted
Baking powder	1½ tsp. (7 mL)
Baking soda	½ tsp. (2 mL)
Salt	½ tsp. (2 mL)
Nutmeg	¼ tsp. (1 mL)

Add flour mixture to creamed mixture alternately with:

Milk	½ cup (125 mL)

Spoon into prepared pan. Bake at 375°F (190°C) for 20 to 25 minutes. Remove from pan and cool on rack.

VARIATION

Plain French Breakfast — Omit grated orange rind and substitute ½ tsp. (2 mL) vanilla extract.

SERVING SUGGESTIONS

Citrus marmalade goes well with either, but Plain French Breakfast is especially tasty with Cinnamon Sugar Topping (see Apple Cinnamon muffin).

anut Butter Bran

Makes: 10 medium
Preheat oven to 400°F (200°C) and prepare pan.

In large bowl cream with electric mixer:

Egg	1
Brown sugar	½ cup (125 mL)
Butter	¼ cup (50 mL)
Peanut butter	½ cup (125 mL), smooth or crunchy

Then add:

All-Bran cereal	1 cup (250 mL)
Milk	1 cup (250 mL)

In smaller bowl combine well:

All-purpose flour	1 cup (250 mL), unsifted
Baking powder	1 Tbsp. (15 mL)
Baking soda	¼ tsp. (1 mL)
Salt	½ tsp. (2 mL)

Combine wet and dry mixtures and fold together gently until just mixed. Spoon into prepared pan. Bake at 400°F (200°C) for 20 to 25 minutes. Remove from pan and cool on rack.

HINT

When made with creamy peanut butter, a good muffin for an infant.

Pineapple Apricot Nut

Makes: 15 medium
Preheat oven to 375°F (190°C) and prepare pan.

In large bowl add and combine well:

Eggs	4
Sugar	¾ cup (175 mL)
Oil	1 cup (250 mL)
Crushed unsweetened pineapple	1 cup (250 mL), undrained
Finely chopped dried apricot	¾ cup (175 mL)
Grated rind of 1 lemon	approx. 1 Tbsp. (15 mL)

In smaller bowl combine well:

All-purpose flour	2 cups (500 mL), unsifted
Baking powder	1 Tbsp. (15 mL)
Baking soda	½ tsp. (2 mL)
Salt	½ tsp. (2 mL)
Chopped almonds, pecans or walnuts	½ cup (125 mL)

Combine wet and dry mixtures and fold together gently until just mixed. Spoon into prepared pan and decorate top of each muffin with a nut half or apricot piece. Bake at 375°F (190°C) for 25 to 30 minutes. Remove from pan and cool on rack.

VARIATIONS

Pineapple Apricot Coconut — Substitute ½ cup (125 mL) flaked or shredded coconut for nuts.
Pineapple Carrot — Substitute 1 cup (250 mL) grated carrot for dried apricots. Add ¼ tsp. (1 mL) allspice to dry mixture.
Pineapple Carrot Orange — Substitute grated rind of 1 orange (approx. 1½ Tbsp.) (22 mL) for the lemon in *Pineapple Carrot*.

Pineapple Cottage Cheese

Makes: 12 medium
Preheat oven to 400°F (200°C) and prepare pan.

In large bowl add and combine well:

Eggs	4
Brown sugar	⅓ cup (75 mL)
Oil	½ cup (125 mL)
Creamed cottage cheese	1 cup (250 mL)
Crushed pineapple	1 cup (250 mL), undrained
Vanilla	1 tsp. (5 mL)

In smaller bowl combine well:

Whole-wheat flour	1 cup (250 mL), unsifted
Cake and pastry flour	1 cup (250 mL), unsifted
Baking powder	1 Tbsp. (15 mL)
Baking soda	½ tsp. (2 mL)
Salt	¼ tsp. (2 mL)
Nutmeg	¼ tsp. (1 mL)

Combine wet and dry mixtures and fold together gently until just mixed. Spoon into prepared pan. Bake at 400°F (200°C) for 20 minutes. Remove from pan and cool on rack.

VARIATION

Fruit Cocktail Cottage Cheese — Substitute 1 cup (250 mL) well-drained fruit cocktail (1 14-oz. or 398-mL can) for crushed pineapple.

SERVING SUGGESTION

A good lunch muffin to accompany a fruit, melon, or avocado salad.

Pumpkin

made with 1/2 c. brn sugar (good

Makes: 12 medium
Preheat oven to 400°F (200°C) and prepare pan.

In large bowl add and combine well:

Egg	1
Brown sugar	⅔ cup (150 mL)
Butter or margarine	⅓ cup (75 mL), melted
Milk	¾ cup (175 mL)
Canned pumpkin	¾ cup (175 mL)
Raisins	½ cup (125 mL)

In smaller bowl combine well:

All-purpose flour	2 cups (500 mL), unsifted
Baking powder	2 tsp. (10 mL)
Baking soda	½ tsp. (2 mL)
Salt	½ tsp. (2 mL)
Cinnamon	½ tsp. (2 mL)
Nutmeg	½ tsp. (2 mL)
Ground ginger	¼ tsp. (1 mL)

Combine wet and dry mixtures and fold together gently until just mixed. Spoon into prepared pan. Bake at 400°F (200°C) for 20 to 25 minutes. Remove from pan and cool on rack.

VARIATION

Add roasted pumpkin seeds to batter and sprinkle additional seeds on top of each muffin.

SERVING SUGGESTION

Try with *Orange Cream Cheese Spread*. Make *Orange Butter* (see *Citrus muffin*); cream equal quantities of cream cheese and *Orange Butter* until light and fluffy.

Pumpkin Orange

Makes: 12 medium
Preheat oven to 400°F (200°C) and prepare pan.

In large bowl add and combine well:

Eggs	2
Sugar	¾ cup (175 mL)
Oil	¼ cup (50 mL)
Apple juice or cider	½ cup (125 mL)
Canned pumpkin	1 cup (250 mL)
Grated rind of 1 orange	approx. 1½ Tbsp. (22 mL)

In smaller bowl combine well:

All-purpose flour	2 cups (500 mL), unsifted
Baking powder	1 Tbsp. (15 mL)
Baking soda	½ tsp. (2 mL)
Salt	½ tsp. (2 mL)
Cinnamon	¼ tsp. (1 mL)
Mace	¼ tsp. (1 mL)
Ground cloves	⅛ tsp. (0.5 mL)
Chopped walnuts or pecans	½ cup (125 mL)

Combine wet and dry mixtures and fold together gently until just mixed. Spoon into prepared pan and decorate top of each muffin with a walnut or pecan half. Bake at 400°F (200°C) for 20 to 25 minutes. Remove from pan and cool on rack.

Rhubarb Cinnamon

Makes: 12 medium
Preheat oven to 375°F (190°C) and prepare pan.

In large bowl add and combine well:

Eggs	2
Sugar	1 cup (250 mL)
Oil	¼ cup (50 mL)
Plain yogurt or buttermilk	½ cup (125 mL)
Vanilla	1 tsp. (5 mL)
Chopped fresh rhubarb	1¾ cup (425 mL), lightly packed

In smaller bowl combine well:

All-purpose flour	2 cups (500 mL), unsifted
Baking powder	2 tsp. (10 mL)
Baking soda	½ tsp. (2 mL)
Salt	½ tsp. (2 mL)
Cinnamon	¼ tsp. (1 mL)

Combine wet and dry mixtures and fold together gently until just mixed. Spoon into prepared pan. Bake at 375°C (190°C) for 25 minutes. Remove from pan and cool on rack.

VARIATION

Rhubarb Orange — Add 1 tsp. (5 mL) grated orange peel. Substitute ¼ tsp. (1 mL) mace for cinnamon.

HINT

Only fresh rhubarb will do; frozen rhubarb is often stringy and produces a soggy batter.

SERVING SUGGESTION

Serve warm with stewed fruit and *Cinnamon Butter* (see *Apple Plus* muffin), or dip hot muffin tops in melted butter and *Orange Sugar* (see *Citrus* muffin).

Rice

Makes: 12 medium
Preheat oven to 400°F (200°C) and prepare pan.

In large bowl add and combine well:

Egg	1
Honey	¼ cup (50 mL)
Oil	2 Tbsp. (30 mL)
Milk	½ cup (125 mL)
Vanilla	1 tsp. (2 mL)
Cooked rice	1 cup (250 mL), lightly packed

In smaller bowl combine well:

All-purpose flour	1 cup (250 mL), unsifted
Baking powder	1 Tbsp. (15 mL)
Baking soda	½ tsp. (2 mL)
Salt	½ tsp. (2 mL)

Combine wet and dry mixtures and fold together gently until just mixed. Spoon into prepared pan and decorate top of each muffin with a walnut or pecan half. Bake at 400°F (200°C) for 15 to 20 minutes. Remove from pan and cool on rack.

VARIATION

Brown Rice — Substitute cooked brown rice for white.

HINT

Rice muffins should be eaten freshly baked as rice dries out when frozen.

SERVING SUGGESTION

A tasty luncheon accompaniment to chicken salad or cold stuffed tomato. Serve for breakfast with *Apple Cinnamon Topping* — slice an apple thinly, toss in cinnamon sugar. Press two or three apple slices on tops of each muffin before baking.

Rise 'n' Shine

Makes: 12 large or 16 medium
Preheat oven to 375°F (190°C) and prepare pan.

In *large bowl add and combine well*:

Eggs	4
Sugar	1 cup (250 mL)
Oil	1 cup (250 mL)
Apple juice	¼ cup (50 mL)
Grated carrot	2 cups (500 mL), lightly packed, 4 medium
Sweetened shredded or flaked coconut	½ cup (125 mL)
Currants or raisins	½ cup (125 mL)
Vanilla	2 tsp. (10 mL)

In *smaller bowl combine well*:

All-purpose flour	2 cups (500 mL), unsifted
Baking powder	1 Tbsp. (15 mL)
Baking soda	1 tsp. (5 mL)
Cinnamon	1 tsp. (5 mL)
Salt	½ tsp. (2 mL)
Chopped walnuts or pecans	½ cup (125 mL)

Combine wet and dry mixtures and fold together gently until just mixed. Spoon into prepared pan and decorate top of each muffin with a walnut or pecan half. Bake at 375°F (190°C) for 25 to 30 minutes. Remove from pan and cool on rack.

VARIATION

Omit chopped walnuts or pecans. Substitute roasted pumpkin seeds or raw sunflower seeds. Sprinkle additional seeds on top.

Rum 'n' Raisin

need sugar too dry

Makes: 8 medium
Preheat oven to 400°F (200°C) and prepare pan.

In large bowl add and combine well:

Egg	1
Sugar	⅓ cup (75 mL)
Butter	½ cup (125 mL), melted
Milk	½ cup (125 mL)
Light rum	¼ cup (50 mL)
Vanilla	1 tsp. (5 mL)
Raisins	½ cup (125 mL)

In smaller bowl combine well:

Cake and pastry flour	1¾ cups (425 mL), unsifted
Baking powder	1½ tsp. (7 mL)
Baking soda	½ tsp. (2 mL)
Salt	¼ tsp. (1 mL)
Nutmeg	¼ tsp. (1 mL)

Combine wet and dry mixtures and fold together gently until just mixed. Spoon into prepared pan. Bake at 400°F (200°C) for 20 minutes. Remove from pan and cool on rack.

VARIATION

Rum 'n' Eggnog — Substitute ½ cup (125 mL) commercial or home-made eggnog for milk, or dissolve 3 Tbsp. (50 mL) eggnog crystals in ½ cup (125 mL) milk.

HINT

You may substitute 1 tsp. (5 mL) rum extract for vanilla, omit rum liquor and change milk to ¾ cup (175 mL).

Sesame Seed

Makes: 12 medium
Preheat oven to 400°F (200°C) and prepare pan.

In large bowl add and combine well:

Eggs	2
Honey	½ cup (125 mL)
Oil	¼ cup (50 mL)
Milk	⅔ cup (150 mL)
Vanilla or almond extract	1 tsp. (5 mL) vanilla, ½ tsp. (2 mL) almond

In smaller bowl combine well:

Cake and pastry flour	1 cup (250 mL), unsifted
Ground sesame seeds	1 cup (250 mL)
Baking powder	1½ tsp. (7 mL)
Baking soda	½ tsp. (2 mL)
Salt	½ tsp. (2 mL)
Sesame seeds	⅔ cups (150 mL), raw

Combine wet and dry mixtures and fold together gently until just mixed. Spoon into prepared pan. Bake at 400°F (200°C) for 20 to 25 minutes. Remove from pan and cool on rack.

VARIATIONS

Sunflower Seed — Substitute 1 cup (250 mL) ground sunflower seeds for ground sesame seeds, and ½ cup (125 mL) whole sunflower seeds for sesame seeds.
Sunflower or Sesame Date — Reduce honey to ½ cup (50 mL). Add ½ cup (125 mL) finely chopped dates to wet mixture.

SERVING SUGGESTION

Make *Honey Orange Butter* — Cream ½ cup (125 mL) unsalted butter together with ½ cup (125 mL) honey and the grated rind of one orange (approx. 1½ Tbsp. or 22 mL). When serving *Honey Orange Butter*, you may wish to reduce honey to ¼ cup (50 mL) in the muffin.

Six-Week Refrigerator Bran

Makes: 48 medium
Preheat oven to 375°F (190°C) and prepare pans.

Mix and allow to cool:

100% Bran Flakes	2 cups (500 mL)
Boiling water	2 cups (500 mL)

In large bowl cream with an electric mixer:

Margarine	2 cups (500 mL)
Brown sugar or white	2 cups (500 mL)
Eggs	5

In smaller bowl combine well:

All-purpose flour	5 cups (1250 mL), unsifted
Baking soda	2 Tbsp. (30 mL)
Salt	½ tsp. (2 mL)

Add flour mixture to creamed mixture alternately with

Buttermilk	1 quart (1000 mL)

Gently fold in:

Bran mixture	as prepared above
All-Bran or Bran Buds cereal	4 cups (1000 mL)

Take a portion of the batter and gently stir in dried fruits or nuts in whatever quantity you wish. Spoon into prepared pans. Bake at 375°F (190°C) for 20 minutes. Let cool a few minutes for easier removal. Remove from pans and cool on rack.

VARIATIONS

Bran Oatmeal — Substitute 4 cups (1000 mL) quick-cooking or regular oatmeal for All-Bran or Bran Buds cereal.
Bran and Grape Nut Cereal — Substitute 2 cups (500 mL) Grape Nut Flakes for Bran Flakes.
Molasses Bran — Substitute ½ cup (125 mL) light molasses plus 1½ cups (375 mL) brown sugar for sugar.

HINT

Keep batter in air-tight containers in refrigerator and fold in fruits and nuts just before baking.

Sour Cream Coffee

Makes: 12 medium
Preheat oven to 375°F (190°C) and prepare pan.

Make filling by rubbing together:

Brown sugar	¼ cup (50 mL)
Finely chopped walnuts or pecans	¼ cup (50 mL)
Cinnamon	½ tsp. (2 mL)

In large bowl cream with electric mixer:

Butter	½ cup (125 mL)
Sugar	½ cup (125 mL)
Eggs	2

Add and combine well:

Sour cream	1 cup (250 mL)
Vanilla	1 tsp. (5 mL)

In smaller bowl combine well:

All-purpose flour	2 cups (500 mL), unsifted
Baking powder	1 tsp. (5 mL)
Baking soda	1 tsp. (5 mL)
Salt	¼ tsp. (1 mL)

Spoon 1 Tbsp. (15 mL) batter into each cup. Sprinkle 1 tsp. (5 mL) filling in the middle of each muffin. Top with 1 Tbsp. (15 mL) batter. Sprinkle remaining filling on top of each muffin. Bake at 375°F (190°C) for 25 minutes. Remove from pan and cool on rack.

HINT

Calorie watchers — replace sour cream with non-fat plain yogurt.

Sweet Potato

Makes: 15 medium
Preheat oven to 400°F (200°C) and prepare pan.

Make a sweet potato purée:
Drain 1 14-oz. (398-mL) can of sweet potato and purée in blender or food processor. Set aside.

In large bowl add and combine well:

Eggs	3
Brown sugar	⅔ cup (150 mL), lightly packed
Butter or margarine	½ cup (125 mL), melted
Sweet potato purée	1¼ cups (300 mL), prepared as above
Milk	½ cup (125 mL)
Vanilla	½ tsp. (5 mL)

In smaller bowl combine well:

All-purpose flour	2 cups (500 mL), unsifted
Baking powder	2 tsp. (10 mL)
Baking soda	½ tsp. (2 mL)
Salt	½ tsp. (2 mL)
Nutmeg	¼ tsp. (1 mL)
Ground cloves	one pinch
Chopped walnuts or pecans	½ cup (125 mL)

Combine wet and dry mixtures and fold together gently until just mixed. Spoon into prepared pan and decorate top of each muffin with a walnut or pecan half. Bake at 400°F (200°C) for 20 minutes. Remove from pan and cool on rack.

VARIATION

Sweet Potato Orange — Substitute the grated rind of 1 orange (approx. 1½ Tbsp. or 22 mL) for vanilla.

SERVING SUGGESTIONS

Serve instead of dinner roll at buffet meal or barbecue. Try with ham, spareribs or sausages. Or make a *Melted Marshmallow Topping* — just 5 minutes before baking is completed, place one large marshmallow on top of each muffin. Return to oven for 5 minutes.

Toasted Wheat Germ and Sesame

Makes: 10 medium
Preheat oven to 400°F (200°C) and prepare pan.

In large bowl add and combine well:

Eggs	2
Brown sugar	½ cup (125 mL)
Oil	½ cup (125 mL)
Vanilla or maple extract	1 tsp. (5 mL) vanilla or ½ tsp. (2 mL) maple

In smaller bowl combine well:

Cake and pastry flour	1 cup (250 mL), unsifted
Toasted wheat germ	1 cup (250 mL)
Baking powder	2 tsp. (10 mL)
Baking soda	½ tsp. (2 mL)
Salt	½ tsp. (2 mL)
Sesame seeds	¼ cup (50 mL), raw

Combine wet and dry mixtures and fold together gently until just mixed. Spoon into prepared pan. Bake at 400°F (200°C) for 20 to 25 minutes. Remove from pan and cool on rack.

VARIATION

Graham Cracker — Omit sesame seeds and substitute graham cracker crumbs for toasted wheat germ. Reduce brown sugar to ¼ cup (50 mL).

SERVING SUGGESTION

Make *Lemon* or *Orange Cream Cheese Spread* — see *Citrus Zucchini/Courgette* or *Pumpkin*.

Twelve-Grain

Makes: 12 medium
Preheat oven to 400°F (200°C) and prepare pan.

Combine and allow to cool:

Twelve-grain cereal	¾ cup (175 mL)
Boiling water	1½ cups (375 mL)
Instant coffee	1 tsp. (5 mL), optional

In large bowl add and combine well:

Egg	1
Brown sugar	¼ cup (50 mL)
Oil	½ cup (125 mL)
Twelve-grain mixture	as prepared above
Vanilla or maple extract	1 tsp. (5 mL)
Chopped dates	¾ cup (175 mL)

In smaller bowl combine well:

Cake and pastry flour	1½ cups (375 mL), unsifted
Baking powder	2 tsp. (10 mL)
Baking soda	½ tsp. (2 mL)
Salt	½ tsp. (2 mL)

Combine wet and dry mixtures and fold together gently until just mixed. Spoon into prepared pan. Bake at 400°F (200°C) for 20 to 25 minutes. Remove from pan and cool on rack.

VARIATION

Cracked Wheat — Substitute ¾ cup (175 mL) cracked wheat for twelve-grain cereal.

HINT

The twelve grains are cracked wheat, rye meal, cornmeal, rolled oats, barley grits, sunflower seeds, sesame seeds, buckwheat groats, flaxseed, millet, rice grits and soya grits. Six-grain cereal is also available and may be substituted.

Whole-Wheat

Makes: 10 medium
Preheat oven to 375°F (190°C) and prepare pan.

In large bowl add and combine well:

Eggs	2	
Honey	¼ cup (50 mL)	
Oil	½ cup (125 mL)	
Milk	¾ cup (175 mL)	
Vanilla	1 tsp. (5 mL)	

In smaller bowl combine well:

Whole-wheat flour	1 cup (250 mL), unsifted
Cake and pastry flour	½ cup (125 mL), unsifted
Baking powder	1½ tsp. (7 mL)
Baking soda	½ tsp. (2 mL)
Salt	½ tsp. (2 mL)

Combine wet and dry mixtures and fold together until just mixed.
Spoon into prepared pan. Bake at 375°F (190°C) for 20 to 25 minutes.

VARIATION

Whole-Wheat Molasses — Substitute 2 Tbsp. (30 mL) light molasses
and 2 Tbsp. (30 mL) honey for ¼ cup (50 mL) honey.

SERVING SUGGESTION

Make *Sunflower Seed Spread* — Cream together until light and fluffy
1 cup (250 mL) ground raw sunflower seeds, ¼ cup (50 mL) peanut
butter, 2 Tbsp. (30 mL) sunflower seed oil, ¼ tsp. (1 mL) seasoned salt.

Whole-Wheat Cranberry Orange

Makes: 24 miniature or 12 medium
Preheat oven to 400°F (200°C) and prepare pan.

In large bowl add and combine well:

Eggs	2
Brown sugar	½ cup (125 mL)
Oil	½ cup (125 mL)
Milk	1 cup (250 mL)
Grated rind of 1 orange	approx. 2 Tbsp. (30 mL)

In smaller bowl combine well:

Whole-wheat flour	2 cups (500 mL), unsifted
Baking powder	1 Tbsp. (15 mL)
Baking soda	½ tsp. (2 mL)
Salt	½ tsp. (2 mL)
Chopped frozen or fresh cranberries	1½ cups (375 mL)

Combine wet and dry mixtures and fold together gently until just mixed. Spoon into prepared pan. Bake at 400°F (200°C) for 20 to 25 minutes. Remove from pan and cool on rack.

VARIATIONS

Whole-Wheat Blueberry Orange — Substitute whole fresh or frozen blueberries for cranberries.
Plain Cranberry or Blueberry Orange — Substitute 1 cup (250 mL) unsifted all-purpose flour plus 1¼ cup (300 mL) unsifted cake and pastry flour for whole-wheat flour.

HINT

Do not defrost frozen blueberries or cranberries before using. Defrosted berries produce a highly discoloured batter.

SERVING SUGGESTION

Make miniatures for holiday parties. Freezes well. Makes attractive Christmas gift.

Whole-Wheat Peach

Makes: 12 medium
Preheat oven to 375°F (190°C) and prepare pan.

In large bowl add and combine well:

Eggs	4
Brown sugar	½ cup (125 mL)
Oil	⅓ cup (75 mL)
Milk	¾ cup (175 mL)
Chopped canned peaches	1 cup (250 mL), well-drained, (1 14-oz. or 398-mL can)
Almond extract	½ tsp. (2 mL)

In smaller bowl combine well:

Whole-wheat flour	1 cup (250 mL), unsifted
Cake and pastry flour	1 cup (250 mL), unsifted
Baking powder	1 Tbsp. (15 mL)
Baking soda	1 tsp. (5 mL)
Salt	¼ tsp. (1 mL)
Chopped almonds or pecans	½ cup (125 mL)

Combine wet and dry mixtures and fold together gently until just mixed. Spoon into prepared pan and decorate top of each muffin with an almond or pecan half. Bake at 375°F (190°C) for 25 to 30 minutes. Remove from pan and cool on rack.

VARIATIONS

Whole-Wheat Apricot — Substitute 1 cup (250 mL) chopped canned apricots (1 14-oz. or 398-mL can) for peaches.
Whole-Wheat Peach or Apricot with Coconut — Reduce cake and pastry flour to ½ cup (125 mL) and add ½ cup (125 mL) unsweetened desiccated coconut to dry mixture.
Whole-Wheat Pear Ginger — Substitute 1 cup (250 mL) canned chopped pears for peaches. Omit almond extract and add 6 to 8 pieces of finely chopped crystallized ginger to dry mixture.

Zucchini/Courgette Spice

Makes: 10 medium
Preheat oven to 400°F (200°C) and prepare pan.

In large bowl add and combine well:

Eggs	2
Brown sugar	⅔ cup (150 mL)
Oil	½ cup (125 mL)
Milk	¼ cup (50 mL)
Vanilla	1 tsp. (5 mL)
Grated unpeeled zucchini/ courgette	1½ cups (375 mL), 2 small

In smaller bowl combine well:

All-purpose flour	1½ cups (375 mL), unsifted
Baking powder	1½ tsp. (7 mL)
Baking soda	½ tsp. (2 mL)
Salt	½ tsp. (2 mL)
Cinnamon	½ tsp. (2 mL)
Nutmeg	¼ tsp. (1 mL)
Chopped walnuts or pecans	½ cup (125 mL)

Combine wet and dry mixtures and fold together gently until just mixed. Spoon into prepared pan and decorate top of each muffin with a walnut or pecan half. Bake at 400°F (200°C) for 20 to 25 minutes. Remove from pan and cool on rack.

VARIATIONS

Carrot Spice — Substitute 1½ cups (375 mL) finely grated carrot for zucchini/courgette. Add ½ cup (125 mL) raisins.
Whole-Wheat Carrot or Zucchini/Courgette — Substitute 1 cup (250 mL) unsifted whole-wheat flour and ½ cup (125 mL) unsifted cake and pastry flour for 1½ cups (375 mL) all-purpose flour.

SERVING SUGGESTION

Make *Cream Cheese Spread* — Mix equal quantities of butter and cream cheese. Whip until light and fluffy.

Savoury Muffins

All Corn

Preheat oven to 400°F (200°C) and prepare pan.

In large bowl add and combine well:

Cornmeal	1 cup (250 mL)
Baking powder	2 tsp. (10 mL)
Baking soda	½ tsp. (2 mL)
Salt	1 tsp. (5 mL)

Add and combine well:

Eggs	2
Corn oil	¼ cup (50 mL)
Sour cream	1 cup (250 mL)
Creamed corn	1 cup (250 mL)

Spoon into prepared pan. Bake at 400°F (200°C) for 20 minutes. Remove from pan and cool on rack.

HINT

Only one bowl is required as there is no flour to incorporate.

SERVING SUGGESTIONS

Serve with peameal bacon or sausages for breakfast, or with ham or chicken for dinner. Excellent with cream of tomato soup.

Caraway Cheese

Makes: 12 medium
Preheat oven to 400°F (200°C) and prepare pan.

In large bowl add and combine well:

Eggs	2
Sugar	¼ cup (50 mL)
Oil	¼ cup (50 mL)
Plain yogurt or buttermilk	¾ cup (175 mL)
Creamed cottage cheese	1 cup (250 mL)
Caraway seeds	1½ tsp. (7 mL), or to taste
Grated lemon rind	1 tsp. (5 mL)

In smaller bowl combine well:

Whole-wheat flour	1 cup (250 mL), unsifted
Cake and pastry flour	1 cup (250 mL), unsifted
Baking powder	2 tsp. (10 mL)
Baking soda	½ tsp. (2 mL)
Salt	½ tsp. (2 mL)

Combine wet and dry mixtures and fold together gently until just mixed. Spoon into prepared pan. Bake at 400°F (200°C) for 20 to 25 minutes. Remove from pan and cool on rack.

VARIATION

Poppy Seed Cheese — Substitute 1½ tsp. (7 mL) poppy seeds for caraway seeds.

SERVING SUGGESTION

Make *Cream Cheese Spread* (see *Zucchini/Courgette Spice* muffin).

Caraway Onion

Makes: 12 medium
Preheat oven to 400°F (200°C) and prepare pan.

In a large frying pan sauté in bacon fat or oil until golden, then cool:

Finely chopped onion	½ cup (125 mL), 1 small
Caraway seeds	1½ tsp. (7 mL), or to taste
Bacon fat or oil	¼ cup (50 mL)

In a large bowl add and combine well:

Egg	1
Light molasses	¼ cup (50 mL)
Milk	1 cup (250 mL)
Onion mixture	as prepared above

In smaller bowl combine well:

Whole-wheat flour	1 cup (250 mL), unsifted
All-purpose flour	1 cup (250 mL), unsifted
Baking powder	1 Tbsp. (15 mL)
Baking soda	½ tsp. (2 mL)
Salt	1 tsp. (5 mL)

Combine wet and dry mixtures and fold together gently until just mixed. Spoon into prepared pan and sprinkle a small amount of caraway seed on each muffin top. Bake at 400°F (200°C) for 20 to 25 minutes. Remove from pan and cool on rack.

VARIATION

Dill Onion — Substitute dill seed for caraway.

SERVING SUGGESTION

Goes well with potato soup and fish.

Caraway Rye

Makes: 10 medium
Preheat oven to 400°F (200°C) and prepare pan.

In *large bowl add and combine well*:

Egg	1
Brown sugar	2 Tbsp. (30 mL)
Oil	¼ cup (50 mL)
Milk	1 cup (250 mL)
Rye flakes	1 cup (250 mL)
Caraway seeds	¾ tsp. (3 mL), or to taste

In *smaller bowl combine well*:

All-purpose flour	1 cup (250 mL), unsifted
Baking powder	2 tsp. (10 mL)
Salt	½ tsp. (2 mL)

Combine wet and dry mixtures and fold together gently until just mixed. Spoon into prepared pan. Bake at 400°F (200°C) for 20 minutes. Remove from pan and cool on rack.

VARIATION

Plain Rye — Omit caraway seeds.

SERVING SUGGESTION

Spread with whipped cream cheese.
   Plain Rye is very tasty with *Parmesan Butter* — Cream together until light and fluffy ½ cup (125 mL) softened butter, ½ cup (125 mL) grated Parmesan cheese, 2 Tbsp. (30 mL) chopped fresh parsley and ½ tsp. (2 mL) onion powder.

Celery

Makes: 12 medium
Preheat oven to 400°F (200°C) and prepare pan.

In large bowl add and combine well:

Eggs	4
Oil	½ cup (125 mL)
Cream of celery soup	1 10-oz. (284-mL) can, undiluted
Chopped celery	1 cup (250 mL), 2 medium stalks
Grated Parmesan cheese	¼ cup (50 mL)
Freshly chopped parsley	2 Tbsp. (30 mL)
Celery salt	¼ tsp. (1 mL)
Onion salt	¼ tsp. (1 mL)

In smaller bowl combine well:

All-purpose flour	2 cups (500 mL), unsifted
Baking powder	2 tsp. (10 mL)
Baking soda	1 tsp. (5 mL)

Combine wet and dry mixtures and fold together gently until just mixed. Spoon into prepared pan. Bake at 400°F (200°C) for 20 minutes. Remove from pan and cool on rack.

SERVING SUGGESTION

Make Parmesan Butter (see Caraway Rye Flake muffin) and serve with cream of tomato soup or serve warm with meatloaf.

Cheese 'n' V-8

Makes: 10 medium
Preheat oven to 400°F (200°C) and prepare pan.

In large bowl add and combine well:

Egg	1
Oil	⅓ cup (75 mL)
V-8 juice	1 cup (250 mL)
Grated old Cheddar	½ cup (125 mL)

In smaller bowl combine well:

All-purpose flour	1¾ cup (425 mL), unsifted
Baking powder	2 tsp. (10 mL)
Baking soda	½ tsp. (2 mL)
Salt	½ tsp. (2 mL)

Combine wet and dry mixtures and fold together gently until just mixed. Spoon into prepared pan. Bake at 400°F (200°C) for 20 minutes. Remove from pan and cool on rack.

SERVING SUGGESTION

Serve with a salad and quiche or omelette for lunch. This muffin adds zest to bland soups such as cream of celery, mushroom or potato.

Cheese with Parsley and Peppers

Makes: 12 medium
Preheat oven to 400°F (200°C) and prepare pan.

In large bowl add and combine well:

Eggs	2
Oil	½ cup (125 mL)
Cheddar cheese soup	1 10-oz. (284-mL) can, undiluted
Chopped green pepper	⅓ cup (75 mL), ½ medium
Chopped fresh parsley	½ cup (125 mL)
Worcestershire sauce	4 dashes

In smaller bowl combine well:

Whole-wheat flour	1 cup (250 mL), unsifted
Cake and pastry flour	1 cup (250 mL), unsifted
Baking powder	1 Tbsp. (15 mL)
Baking soda	¼ tsp. (1 mL)
Salt or seasoned salt	½ tsp. (2 mL)

Combine wet and dry mixtures and fold together gently until just mixed. Spoon into prepared pan. Bake at 400°F (200°C) for 20 to 25 minutes. Remove from pan and cool on rack.

VARIATION

Cheese with Parsley and Onion — Substitute 2 Tbsp. (30 mL) dried parsley and 2 Tbsp. (30 mL) dried onion flakes for fresh parsley and peppers.

HINT

Before baking, place a small piece of cheese on each muffin top for extra cheese flavour.

SERVING SUGGESTION

Excellent accompaniment for a variety of soups — cream of chicken or potato, gazpacho, tomato or minestrone. Try serving with chili con carne.

Corn Niblet

Makes: 12 medium
Preheat oven to 400°F (200°C) and prepare pan.

In large bowl add and combine well:

Eggs	2
Butter or margarine	½ cup (125 mL), melted
Buttermilk	1½ cups (375 mL)
Cornmeal	1 cup (250 mL)
Whole kernel corn	1 cup (250 mL), 1 12-oz. (375-mL) can

In smaller bowl combine well:

All-purpose flour	1 cup (250 mL), unsifted
Sugar	1½ Tbsp. (22 mL)
Baking powder	2 tsp. (10 mL)
Baking soda	1 tsp. (5 mL)
Salt	½ tsp. (2 mL)

Combine wet and dry mixtures and fold together gently until just mixed. Spoon into prepared pan. Bake at 400°F (200°C) for 25 minutes. Remove from pan and cool on rack.

VARIATION

Bacon Corn Niblet — Omit salt. Chop 10 slices of bacon, fry until crisp and set aside. Pour bacon fat into measuring cup and add oil to measure ½ cup (125 mL). Put into wet mixture. Fold bacon into batter at last moment.

SERVING SUGGESTION

Good with eggs, ham or chicken. Take to a potluck supper instead of rolls.

Cornmeal Sage

Makes: 14 medium
Preheat oven to 400°F (200°C) and prepare pan.

Mix and allow to soak for 10 *minutes:*

Cornmeal	1½ cups (375 mL)
Buttermilk	2 cups (500 mL)

In large bowl add and combine well:

Eggs	3
Sugar	1 Tbsp. (15 mL)
Butter or margarine	½ cup (125 mL), melted
Fresh or dried sage	1 Tbsp. (15 mL) fresh, 1 tsp. (5 mL) dried

In smaller bowl combine well:

All-purpose flour	1½ cups (375 mL), unsifted
Baking powder	1 Tbsp. (15 mL)
Baking soda	1 tsp. (5 mL)
Salt	1½ tsp. (7 mL)

Combine wet and dry mixtures and fold together gently until just mixed. Spoon into prepared pan. Bake at 400°F (200°C) for 20 minutes. Remove from pan and cool on rack.

VARIATION

Cornmeal Marjoram — Substitute 1 Tbsp. (15 mL) fresh marjoram or 1 tsp. (5 mL) dried for sage.

SERVING SUGGESTIONS

With ground beef casserole, roast chicken or a hearty stew.

Cornmeal Tomato

Makes: 12 medium
Preheat oven to 400°F (200°C) and prepare pan.

Combine and let soak for 10 minutes:

Cornmeal	1 cup (250 mL)
Canned tomatoes	1 14-oz. (398-mL) can, including liquid

In large bowl add and combine well:

Eggs	2
Brown sugar	2 Tbsp. (30 mL)
Oil	½ cup (125 mL)
Cornmeal mixture	as prepared above
Dried sweet basil	¾ tsp. (3 mL), or to taste

In smaller bowl combine well:

All-purpose flour	1½ cups (375 mL), unsifted
Baking powder	1 Tbsp. (15 mL)
Baking soda	½ tsp. (2 mL)
Salt	1 tsp. (5 mL)
Garlic powder	¼ tsp. (1 mL)

Combine wet and dry mixtures and fold together gently until just mixed. Spoon into prepared pan. Bake at 400°F (200°C) for 25 minutes. Remove from pan and cool on rack.

VARIATION

Cornmeal with Tomato Bits — Substitute 1¼ cups (300 mL) milk for canned tomatoes. Reduce oil to ¼ cup (50 mL) and add 1 cup (250 mL) peeled, seeded chopped fresh tomatoes to wet mixture.

HINT

For best flavour, muffin must be served very warm with butter. Use only fresh tomatoes in season for variation.

SERVING SUGGESTION

Try with clam or fish chowder.

Cottage Cheese Dill

Makes: 12 medium
Preheat oven to 400°F (200°C) and prepare pan.

In *large bowl add and combine well*:

Egg	1
Oil	¼ cup (50 mL)
Milk	½ cup (125 mL)
Creamed cottage cheese	1 cup (250 mL), small-curd
Fresh young dill	2 Tbsp. (30 mL), finely chopped
Chopped green onion	2 Tbsp. (30 mL)
Worcestershire sauce	½ tsp. (2 mL)
Seasoned salt	½ tsp. (2 mL)

In *smaller bowl combine well*:

All-purpose flour	2 cups (500 mL), unsifted
Baking powder	1 Tbsp. (15 mL)

Combine wet and dry mixtures and fold together gently until just mixed. Spoon into prepared pan. Bake at 400°F (200°C) for 25 to 30 minutes. Remove from pan and cool on rack.

VARIATION

Potato with Dill-Onion-Parsley — Substitute 1 10-oz. (284-mL) can of cream of potato soup for cheese and purée in blender or food processor. Add 2 Tbsp. (30 mL) chopped fresh parsley to wet mixture.

SERVING SUGGESTION

Good with fresh asparagus or tomato soup, or serve for brunch with scrambled eggs and corned beef hash.

Creamy Corn Cheese

Makes: 12 medium
Preheat oven to 400°F (200°C) and prepare pan.

In large bowl add and combine well:

Egg	1
Corn oil	¼ cup (50 mL)
Sour cream	¼ cup (50 mL)
Creamed corn	1¼ cups (300 mL), 1 10-oz. (284-mL) can
Grated old or medium Cheddar	¾ cup (175 mL)

In smaller bowl combine well:

All-purpose flour	1½ cups (375 mL), unsifted
Sugar	1 Tbsp. (15 mL)
Baking powder	1½ tsp. (7 mL)
Baking soda	½ tsp. (2 mL)
Salt	½ tsp. (2 mL)

Combine wet and dry mixtures and fold together gently until just mixed. Spoon into prepared pan. Bake at 400°F (200°C) for 20 minutes. Remove from pan and cool on rack.

VARIATION

Kernel Corn Cheese — Substitute 1 cup (250 mL) whole kernel corn (drained) for creamed corn. Substitute 1 cup (250 mL) buttermilk for sour cream.

HINT

To grate fresh cheese more easily, first freeze for 30 to 40 minutes.

SERVING SUGGESTION

A fast supper when served with fried sausages and bean salad.

Ham Nugget in Corn

Makes: 12 medium
Preheat oven to 400°F (200°C) and prepare pan.

In large bowl add and combine well:

Eggs	2
Oil	½ cup (125 mL)
Creamed corn	1½ cups (375 mL), 1 14-oz. (398-mL) can

In smaller bowl combine well:

Whole-wheat flour	1 cup (250 mL), unsifted
All-purpose flour	1 cup (250 mL), unsifted
Baking powder	1 Tbsp. (15 mL)
Salt	½ tsp. (2 mL)
Cubes of ham	12 ½-inch cubes

Combine wet and dry mixtures and fold together gently until just mixed. Spoon into prepared pan and press one ½-inch cube of ham into centre of each muffin. Bake at 400°F (200°C) for 20 to 25 minutes. Remove from pan and cool on rack.

VARIATION

Cheddar Nugget in Corn — Substitute cubes of Cheddar for ham.

HINT

Eat *Cheddar Nugget in Corn* muffin warm and freshly baked. Melted Cheddar cheese becomes tough when cooled.

SERVING SUGGESTION

Children enjoy finding the "nugget". Chicken noodle soup goes well with these muffins.

Onion Parsley

Makes: 12 medium
Preheat oven to 400°F (200°C) and prepare pan.

In large bowl add and combine well:

Egg	1
Oil	¼ cup (50 mL)
Milk	1 cup (250 mL)
Finely chopped green onion	⅓ cup (75 mL)
Finely chopped fresh parsley	⅓ cup (75 mL)

In smaller bowl combine well:

All-purpose flour	2 cups (500 mL), unsifted
Sugar	1 Tbsp. (15 mL)
Baking powder	1 Tbsp. (15 mL)
Salt	1½ tsp. (7 mL)

Combine wet and dry mixtures and fold together gently until just mixed. Spoon into prepared pan. Bake at 400°F (200°C) for 20 minutes. Remove from pan and cool on rack.

HINT

Snip fresh parsley, dill, chives or other fresh herbs with kitchen shears.

SERVING SUGGESTION

Make *Cheddar Butter* — Cream together until light and fluffy ½ cup (125 mL) softened butter, ½ cup (125 mL) grated mild or medium Cheddar cheese, 2 Tbsp. (30 mL) chopped fresh parsley.

Parmesan

Makes: 12 medium
Preheat oven to 400°F (200°C) and prepare pan.

In large bowl add and combine well:

Eggs	2
Oil	½ cup (125 mL)
Milk	¾ cup (175 mL)

In smaller bowl combine well:

Whole-wheat flour	1 cup (250 mL), unsifted
Cake and pastry flour	1 cup (250 mL), unsifted
Grated Parmesan cheese	½ cup (125 mL)
Sugar	1 Tbsp. (15 mL)
Baking powder	1 Tbsp. (15 mL)
Garlic salt	½ tsp. (2 mL)
Onion salt	½ tsp. (2 mL)

Combine wet and dry mixtures and fold together gently until just mixed. Spoon into prepared pan. Bake at 400°F (200°C) for 20 to 25 minutes. Remove from pan and cool on rack.

VARIATION

Zucchini/Courgette Parmesan — Reduce milk to ¼ cup (50 mL). Add 1 cup (250 mL) freshly grated zucchini/courgette, unpeeled, to wet mixture.

HINT

Use good quality Parmesan.

SERVING SUGGESTION

Goes well with salads or Italian dishes.

Glossary

Carob: A chocolate substitute available in health food stores. Also known as "St. John's Bread," named after St. John the Baptist who was reported to have survived on carob in the desert. Available in powder or chip form, it is caffeine-free and contains valuable nutrients. Since raw carob powder contains 46% natural sugar, when substituting for chocolate, less sugar is required.

Chocolate/Cocoa: Both chocolate and cocoa come from the hulled bean of the tropical tree *Theobroma* (Food of the Gods). Chocolate liquor is extracted from the beans and molded into solid cakes. Both chocolate and cocoa are made from these cakes.

Sweet chocolate is composed of melted bitter chocolate, cocoa butter, finely milled sugar, milk and vanilla. Semi-sweet chocolate is composed of 60% bitter chocolate and 40% sugar.

Dry unsweetened cocoa powder varies in fat content from 10% in regular cocoa to 24% in Dutch-type breakfast cocoa. Instant cocoa is precooked with an emulsifier which causes it to dissolve easily in liquid. Its 80% sugar content makes it undesirable for baking.

Flour: There are wheat flours and non-wheat flours. Wheat flours can be categorized as hard or soft, depending on their gluten content. Gluten is a protein substance which helps the flour rise during baking. Low gluten flours should be combined with high gluten flours for best results.

Some wheat flours are — all-purpose, cake and pastry, gluten, graham, enriched, cracked wheat, whole wheat, durum, semolina, farina.

Non-wheat flours have no gluten and require more leavening than wheat flours. They should be combined with wheat flours for best results.

Some non-wheat flours are — barley, rye, potato, rice, ground rolled oats, corn, soya.

All-purpose A blend of hard and soft wheats with a high gluten content.
Barley The finely milled kernel of barley and much like rye flour in texture and moistness.

Cake and pastry A finely milled soft wheat flour with a low gluten content. Gives a delicate texture. Whole-wheat cake and pastry flour is also available.

Corn flour Made from finely ground kernels of corn. Produces a lighter corn flavour than cornmeal which is coarsely ground dried corn.

Farina Made from durum wheat after the germ and bran have been removed.

Gluten A high-protein hard wheat flour with most of the starch removed.

Graham A type of whole-wheat flour in which the bran is coarsely ground. Sometimes called whole kernel flour, it may be used interchangeably with whole-wheat.

Instant Ground to a powder and gives a different texture to baking. Some have a higher percentage of gluten and could toughen the muffin.

Rye A heavy flour with a low gluten content, milled from rye grain.

Self-raising Contains baking powder. 1 cup (250 mL) self-raising flour equals 1 cup (250 mL) all-purpose flour plus 1 tsp. (5 mL) baking powder.

Semolina Made from hard wheat durum flour.

Soya Made from ground soy beans. High in protein and low in fat with extremely low gluten content. Has slightly bitter taste — use sparingly.

Triticale A cross between rye and wheat, has a high protein content and a delicious rye-like flavour.

Unbleached A hard wheat bread flour, high in gluten content. Not interchangeable with all-purpose flour in fine baking. A mixture of ¾ cup (175 mL) unbleached plus ¼ cup (50 mL) cake and pastry equals 1 cup (250 mL) all-purpose. Has a shorter shelf life than bleached flours and should be refrigerated. Contains nutrients which are destroyed in the bleaching process. In bleached or enriched flour these nutrients are replaced synthetically.

Whole-wheat Made from the kernel of the wheat and includes the wheat germ and bran. Should be stored in the refrigerator.

Wheat germ Made from the kernel of the wheat grain. Should be stored in the refrigerator. Rich in B-complex and E vitamins, adds a nutty texture to muffins.

Milk powder: Instant is usually non-fat. Non-instant is available as non-fat, whole, buttermilk or soy.

Molasses: For optimum flavour, molasses should replace no more than half of the sweetening power in a recipe.
There are 3 types of molasses —
Unsulphured — manufactured from the juice of the sun-ripened cane.
Sulphured — by-product of sugar.
Blackstrap — waste product of sugar.

Oils: There are nut oils and vegetable oils. Nut oils do not react well to heat and therefore are not suitable for baking. Use vegetable oils pressed from seeds and fruits such as corn, cottonseed, olive, soybean, sesame, sunflower and safflower. Oils are 100% fat and should not be substituted measure for measure for butter. There is 20% more fat in oil; therefore in substituting, adjust accordingly (e.g. ⅓ cup (75 mL) butter for ¼ cup (50 mL) oil). Vegetable shortening, however, may be substituted for butter in equal amounts.

Index

Oatmeal Cranberry   28
Poppy Seed Cheese   75
Red Jam Puffins   46
Rhubarb Cinnamon   59
Rhubarb Orange   59
Six-Week Refrigerator Bran   64
Whole-Wheat Maple Nut   47

Butternut Squash
Butternut Squash   29

Butterscotch
Maple Butterscotch Chip   34

Caraway
Caraway Cheese   75
Caraway Onion   76
Caraway Rye   77

Carob
Banana Carob   21
Banana Carob Chip   21
Carob Chip   30
Carob Orange   30

Carrot
Apple Carrot   15
Banana Carrot   22
Buttery Carrot   31
Carrot Spice   72
Pineapple Carrot   55
Pineapple Carrot Orange   55
Rise 'n' Shine   61
Whole-Wheat Carrot Spice   72

Celery
Celery   78

Cheddar
Apple Cheddar   31
Bacon Cheddar   31
Buttery Carrot   31
Cheddar   31
Cheddar Nugget in Corn   86
Cheese 'n' V-8   79
Cheese with Parsley and
    Onion   80
Cheese with Parsley and
    Peppers   80
Creamy Corn Cheese   85
Date Cheese   31
Kernel Corn Cheese   85

Cherry
Cherry Almond or Pecan   32
Cherry Pineapple   33

Chocolate
Banana Chocolate Chip   21
Chocolate Chip Coconut   37
Chocolate Chocolate Chip   34
Chocolate Coconut   37
Chocolate Ginger Nut   44
Chocolate Orange   30
Chocolate Peanut Butter Chip   34
Mocha Almond   48

Citrus
Citrus (Lemon Orange)   35
Citrus Zucchini/Courgette   36

Coconut
Banana Coconut   23
Carob Coconut   37
Chocolate Coconut   37
Chocolate Chip Coconut   37
Coconut   37
Oatmeal Coconut   49
Pineapple Apricot Coconut   55
Rise 'n' Shine   61
Whole-Wheat Apricot with
    Coconut   71
Whole-Wheat Peach with
    Coconut   71

Corn
All Corn   74
Bacon Corn Niblet   81
Corn Niblet   81
Creamy Corn Cheese   85
Ham Nugget in Corn   86
Kernel Corn Cheese   85

Cornmeal
All Corn   74
Bacon Corn Niblet   81
Corn Niblet   81
Corn Wheat Germ   38
Cornmeal Marjoram   82
Cornmeal Sage   82
Cornmeal Tomato   83
Cornmeal with Preserves   38
Cornmeal with Tomato Bits   83

Cottage Cheese
Caraway Cheese   75
Cottage Cheese Dill   84
Fruit Cocktail Cottage Cheese   56
Pineapple Cottage Cheese   56
Poppy Seed Cheese   75

Courgette
See Zucchini

Sour Cream
Sour Cream Coffee   65

Spreads
Cream Cheese   72
Lemon Cream Cheese   36
Orange Cream Cheese   57
Sunflower   69

Strawberry
Red Jam Puffins   46

Sunflower
Sunflower Seed   64
Sunflower Date   64

Sweet Potato
Sweet Potato   66
Sweet Potato Orange   66

Tomato
Cheese 'n' V-8   74
Cornmeal Tomato   83
Cornmeal with Tomato Bits   83

Toppings
Apple Cinnamon   60
Cinnamon Crumble   15
Cinnamon Sugar   16

Melted Marshmallow   66

Twelve-Grain
Twelve-Grain   68

Wheat Flakes
Apple Wheat   17
Buttermilk Bran Wheat Flakes   27

Wheat Germ
Apple Plus   18
Blueberry Bran Wheat Germ   26
Buttermilk Bran Wheat Germ   27
Corn Wheat Germ   38
Cornmeal with Preserves   38
Cranberry Bran Wheat Germ   26
Flourless Bran   43
Oatmeal Coconut   49
Orange   52
Toasted Wheat Germ and
   Sesame   67

Zucchini
Citrus Zucchini/Courgette   36
Whole-Wheat Zucchini/
   Courgette   72
Zucchini/Courgette Parmesan   88
Zucchini/Courgette Spice   72